The Campus History Series

US COAST GUARD

ACADEMY

The Campus History Series

US COAST GUARD

ACADEMY

CAPT. JEFFREY D. HARTMAN, USCG (RETIRED)

ARCADIA
PUBLISHING

Copyright © 2020 by Capt. Jeffrey D. Hartman, USCG (Retired)
ISBN 978-1-4671-0547-7

Published by Arcadia Publishing
Charleston, South Carolina

Printed in the United States of America

Library of Congress Control Number: 2020934432

For all general information, please contact Arcadia Publishing:
Telephone 843-853-2070
Fax 843-853-0044
E-mail sales@arcadiapublishing.com
For customer service and orders:
Toll-Free 1-888-313-2665

Visit us on the Internet at www.arcadiapublishing.com

This book is dedicated to those Coast Guard Academy graduates who are the Long Blue Line, who have gone before, who are there, and who will come after.

CONTENTS

ACKNOWLEDGMENTS

My great appreciation to all those who assisted with pictures and information, including my classmate Rev. Steve Ulmer and the Coast Guard Academy Alumni Association, especially Melissa Yuhas, assistant director of communication, and the association president, Capt. Andrea Marcille, US Coast Guard (retired; class of 1989), without whose support this project never would have been possible. Many of the vintage pictures were scanned from the Coast Guard Academy's *Tide Rips* class yearbooks. The courtesy lines for these pictures list the *Tide Rips* year of publication. I am especially indebted to Paul Duddy for his assistance. Finally, thanks to my daughter Nicole Clark for her proofing and assistance with pictures.

INTRODUCTION

Speaking at the Coast Guard Academy commencement in 1988, Pres. Ronald Reagan said,

> The fact is many young people have trouble choosing their life's work. . . . But I know what I would say to young people who told me they were torn between different careers. If they said they wanted to help people in distress, guard our borders, conserve fisheries, battle drug smugglers, enforce maritime law, test their courage against stormy seas, defend America in times of war, and wear proudly each day the uniform of this great country—then I would tell them just one thing: I would tell them. Join the Coast Guard.

Joining the Coast Guard can be accomplished in several ways. Enlistment is one way for those who want to serve in any of 24 enlisted specialties. Officers are obtained in one of three ways. The first is a direct commission for an officer transferring from another armed service, such as an US Army aviator. Direct commissions are also available for qualified lawyers and graduates of federal or state maritime academies. The second way is to attend the 17-week Officer Candidate School for those with college degrees. The third way is to attend the Coast Guard Academy in New London, Connecticut. This book is about that third way.

Preparing officers for the Coast Guard is no easy task, as it is a complex organization. It all started with Alexander Hamilton, the first secretary of the treasury. In 1790, Hamilton convinced Congress to approve funding for 10 small sailing ships called cutters to enforce the customs laws in the new nation's ports. This was the beginning of the Coast Guard, which was then known as the Revenue Cutter Service. The first mission of what would later become the Coast Guard was the enforcement of laws and treaties, and its home was the Treasury Department. Coast Guard ships have been called cutters ever since. The officers for the Revenue Cutter Service were obtained by political appointment.

In 1831, the revenue cutter *Gallatin* was directed to patrol the coast looking for mariners in distress. This was the beginning of the mission known as search and rescue. The next mission added was the Lighthouse Service in 1845. This mission grew into the aids to navigation mission, which entails nearly 100,000 short-range aids such as lighthouses, buoys, beacons, ranges, radar reflecting devices, and sound signals. In addition, 11 vessel traffic systems are manned and operated by the Coast Guard, as are all the electronic aids to navigation, which are worldwide in scope.

The boating safety mission started with the passage of the Motorboat Act in 1910. This was followed in 1914 by the International Ice Patrol being started by international agreement following the *Titanic* disaster, and it was again assigned to the Coast Guard. The next year, in 1915, the Life-Saving Service was combined with the Revenue Marine to become the Coast Guard.

The military preparedness mission had been a part of the service from its beginning; the Revenue Service participated in the Quasi-War with France in 1801 and was ordered into the Navy for the War of 1812. In 1917, the service was formally transferred from the Treasury Department into the Navy for World War I. One-third of the author's class of 1963 served in Vietnam, earning 14 Bronze Stars and three Silver Stars.

Living marine resources have long been a mission of the Coast Guard. In 1932, the United States signed the Whaling Convention along with 21 other nations, and the Coast Guard was assigned enforcement responsibilities. Later that same year, the Northern Pacific Halibut Act was passed by Congress and again given to the Coast Guard to enforce. A tremendous increase in the mission was occasioned by the passage of the Fisheries Conservation Management Act in 1976. This gave the Coast Guard the responsibility for fisheries enforcement of primarily foreign fisheries vessels in US waters out to 200 miles, an area known as the economic enforcement zone (EEZ). In Alaska alone, the EEZ amounts to 900,000 square miles of ocean that must be patrolled. Given that enforcement requires boarding foreign vessels and inspecting their fishing logs and catches, this mission is complex and fraught with potential for international confrontations.

In 1940, Pres. Franklin D. Roosevelt invoked the Espionage Act of 1917, giving the Coast Guard responsibilities for ports and waterway security. Following the Pearl Harbor attack, war was declared, transferring the Coast Guard into the US Navy. During World War II, the Coast Guard expanded to a peak of 214,000 members, 90 percent of whom were reservists. The women's arm was established in 1942 as the SPARS—the name was derived from a combination of the first letters of the Coast Guard motto: "Semper Paratus, Always Ready." That same year, the Bureau of Navigation and Steamboat Inspection was transferred to the Coast Guard, establishing the mission of marine safety. This mission is a large one, giving the Coast Guard responsibility for virtually all aspects of the maritime industry, including the approval of plans and construction of all ships in US shipyards, licensing of merchant marine sailors, operation of all US ports, and operating offices in foreign ports doing business with the United States.

In 1967, the Coast Guard left its traditional home in the Treasury Department and became part of the Department of Transportation. The Coast Guard was now responsible for the operation of all US icebreakers in Arctic and Antarctic waters in a mission called ice operations. The Coast Guard's law enforcement responsibilities have been increased over the years with the addition of the missions of drug interdiction, migrant interdiction, and other law enforcement. Marine environmental protection responsibilities greatly increased with the passage of the Water Quality Improvement Act in 1970 and the Oil Pollution Act of 1990, which came about as a result of the *Exxon Valdez* oil spill in 1988.

Following the 2001 attack on the World Trade Center, in 2003, the Department of Homeland Security was established. The Coast Guard, along with 21 other agencies, was transferred into what became the third-largest governmental agency. The increasing threat of cyberterrorism threatens many of the Coast Guard missions that rely on advanced technology. All of this had an impact on the academy and how it must prepare its graduates to be ready to hit the decks running upon entering the fleet.

One

PURPOSE

Capt. Kurt Colella, PhD, PE, the current dean of academics and a 1981 graduate of the academy, stated:

> The US Coast Guard Academy is a place that offers a four-year experience filled with exciting challenges, physical, and professional growth of our future Coast Guard leadership. With a student-to-faculty ratio of approximately eight to one, our mantra is to develop a professional relationship with each and every cadet that supports their development and unlocks their potential.

The Coast Guard Academy is dedicated to graduating officers who are prepared to meet the needs of the service. To accomplish this, the academy has four basic objectives: 1) to provide, by precept and example, an environment that embraces the Coast Guard's core values of honor, respect, and devotion to duty; 2) to provide a sound undergraduate education in a field of interest to the Coast Guard; 3) to provide leadership education; and 4) to provide professional training that enables graduates to step into their responsibilities and duties as junior officers.

Vice Adm. Harry G. Hamlet, class of 1896, was the seventh commandant of the Coast Guard, serving in that role from 1932 to 1936. In 1928, he was appointed the superintendent of the Coast Guard Academy. He wrote the Creed of the United States Coast Guardsman:

I am proud to be a United States Coast Guardsman.
I revere that long line of expert seamen who by their devotion to duty and sacrifice of self have made it possible for me to be a member of a service honored and respected, in peace and in war, throughout the world.
I never, by word or deed, will bring reproach upon the fair name of my service, nor permit others to do so unchallenged.
I will cheerfully and willingly obey all lawful orders.
I will always be on time to relieve, and shall endeavor to do more, rather than less, than my share.
I will always be at my station, alert and standing to my duties.
I shall, as far as I am able, bring to my seniors solutions, not problems.
I shall live joyously but always with the regard for the rights and privileges of others.
I shall endeavor to be a model citizen in the community in which I live.
I shall sell life dearly to an enemy of my country but give it freely to rescue those in peril.
With God's help, I shall endeavor to be one of his noblest works:
A United States Coast Guardsman.

The Mission of the
United States Coast Guard Academy

To graduate young men and women with sound bodies, stout hearts, and alert minds, with a liking for the sea and its lore, and with that high sense of honor, loyalty, and obedience which goes with trained initiative and leadership; well-grounded in seamanship, the sciences, and the amenities, and strong in the resolve to be worthy of the traditions of commissioned officers in the United States Coast Guard in the service of their country and humanity.

VADM Harry G. Hamlet
1929

MISSION STATEMENT. This mission statement is mounted in the lobby of Chase Hall, the residence of the academy cadets. This mission was summarized and promulgated by Vice Adm. Harry G. Hamlet in 1929, while he was the superintendent of the academy. It was modified in 1976 with the words "and women" when the academy became the first US military academy to accept women. (Author's collection.)

TO GRADUATE YOUNG MEN AND WOMEN. Pictured is graduation day for the 93 all-male members of the class of 1963. Every four years, the president of the United States officiates over the graduation. Pres. Lyndon B. Johnson was the honored guest at the graduation in 1964. (Courtesy of Steve Ulmer.)

WITH SOUND BODIES. Cadet Hayley Feindel (class of 2012), conference champion softball pitcher, holds 17 school records, including a single-season ERA of 0.56 and the NCAA D3 all-time strikeout record of 1,457. In 2017, she was inducted into the Coast Guard Academy Hall of Fame. (Courtesy of Paul Duddy.)

STOUT HEARTS. Bob Leggett (class of 1963) makes one of his shots. Leggett was the all-time basketball point leader in academy history when he graduated. He also pitched the first no-hitter for the academy. Following a decorated tour in Vietnam, he earned a doctorate in economics from Lehigh University and had a 30-year career with the CIA, where he focused on Soviet economics. He was selected as a distinguished graduate in 2013. (1963 *Tide Rips*.)

ALERT MINDS. Note that these students are using slide rules in lieu of calculators. Each cadet now gets his or her own computer. Technology is continually changing, and the academy changes with it. (Courtesy of Steve Ulmer.)

WITH A LIKING FOR THE SEA AND ITS LORE. "One hand for the ship and one hand for yourself." These cadets are reefing sails on the *Eagle*. The time spent on the *Eagle* is a great experience, especially for those who have not been to sea. It quickly gives one a feeling for the traditions of the sea and the importance of paying attention to the weather. (Courtesy of Steve Ulmer.)

WITH THAT HIGH SENSE OF HONOR, LOYALTY, AND OBEDIENCE. Pictured here is the 1953 color guard. Military drill is an important aspect of the training at the Coast Guard Academy. The color guard leads the procession of cadet companies in passing in review. (1953 *Tide Rips*.)

WELL-GROUNDED IN SEAMANSHIP, THE SCIENCES, AND HUMANITIES. These students are manning the helm on the *Eagle* in heavy weather. Cadets spend part of each summer on the *Eagle*. Long cruises under sail at the start of third-class year and first-class year are a special and unique component of training at the academy. (Courtesy of Steve Ulmer.)

WORTHY OF TRADITIONS OF COMMISSIONED OFFICERS OF THE US COAST GUARD. This picture was taken as the national anthem played at homecoming in 2018 during the five-year class walk-on before the football game. (Author's collection.)

IN THE SERVICE OF THEIR COUNTRY AND HUMANITY. This HH-65 was utilized for training and is shown deploying a rescue swimmer. A portion of each graduating class is sent to flight training with the US Navy and Marines in Pensacola, Florida. The Coast Guard operates 24 air stations with around 210 fixed- and rotary-wing aircraft. The Coast Guard has the highest percentage of aviators in the officer corps among the US armed services. (Author's collection.)

Two

PLACE

In 1876, the chief of the Revenue Cutter Bureau, Summer I. Kimball, established the first academy, known as the Revenue Cutter School of Instruction, afloat on the revenue cutter *Dobbin* with eight cadets and three instructors. Kimball had long been dissatisfied with the system of the politically based appointment of revenue cutter (R/C) officers. He felt that aspiring officers should have a deep interest in and enthusiasm for a life at sea and that the best way to learn seamanship and navigation was to have them spend extended periods afloat with competent instructors. The *Dobbin*, with its crew and eight cadets, sailed on its first practice cruise on May 24, 1877. Among the cadets—and one of the first to get seasick—was Worth G Ross, who later became the commandant of the Coast Guard.

The new R/C *Salmon P. Chase* relieved the *Dobbin* in 1878. Like the *Dobbin*, the *Chase* had her homeport in New Bedford. The *Chase* was named after Abraham Lincoln's secretary of the treasury, Salmon Portland Chase, and had been specifically designed by Kimball to be a training ship for a dozen cadets. In 1895, the ship was dry-docked, cut in half, and lengthened by 40 feet to enable her to accommodate 25 cadets. Between 1890 and 1894, the school was suspended, with all the officers for the Revenue Cutter Service coming from the Naval Academy at Annapolis due to a surplus of graduates from that academy.

In 1900, the School of Instruction of the Revenue Cutter Service came ashore when it moved into a building at Curtis Bay. The corps of cadets at the time had 40 members, and the faculty had seven instructors. The *Chase* remained a training ship from 1878 until she was replaced by the R/C *Itasca*, a former Navy training ship, in 1907. At 190 feet, the *Itasca* was a barquentine-rigged cutter. In addition to the sails, the *Itasca* had modern equipment and a triple-expansion steam engine. The *Itasca* was replaced in 1922 with the R/C *Alexander Hamilton*, which remained the training ship until 1930.

In 1910, the school that was to become the US Coast Guard Academy moved to the New London, Connecticut, area when the War Department turned over to the service the historic Fort Trumbull located on the banks of the Thames River. Parts of Fort Trumbull dated back to the Revolutionary War and left much to be desired.

One year before its move, the academy's curriculum was increased to four years to make it compatible with West Point and Annapolis. The academy left Fort Trumbull in 1932 and moved to its current location on 100 acres of land, obtained from the City of New London, on the west bank of the Thames River.

THE TOPSAIL SCHOONER R/C *DOBBIN*. This was the first home of the Revenue Cutter School of Instruction in 1876. Named for Pres. Franklin Pierce's secretary of the navy, James Cochrane Dobbin, the *Dobbin* had a length of 93 feet, 9 inches; a beam of 22 feet, 6 inches; and drew 9 feet, 9 inches, of water. She had a complement of 13 officers and men. (Donald Canney, *US Coast Guard and Revenue Cutters, 1790–1935*, Annapolis: Naval Institute Press, 1995.)

R/C *SALMON P. CHASE*. This was the home of the Revenue Cutter School of Instruction beginning in 1878. The cutter was specifically built for the corps of cadets. Named for Pres. Abraham Lincoln's secretary of the treasury, the *Chase* was 115.4 feet long until 1895, when the vessel was cut in two and 40 feet were added to its length to make more room for cadets. The *Chase* had a beam of nearly 25 feet and a draft of 12 feet. (Donald Canney, *US Coast Guard and Revenue Cutters, 1790–1935*, Annapolis: Naval Institute Press, 1995.)

CADETS AT FORT TRUMBULL. In 1910, the War Department turned over Fort Trumbull to the Revenue Cutter Service, and the Revenue Cutter School of Instruction was located here until it was moved to its current location in 1932. Many of the fort's buildings were constructed in the days of the Revolutionary War, and their age was apparent. (1935 *Tide Rips*.)

EARLY PICTURE OF THE US COAST GUARD ACADEMY. While it was located at Fort Trumbull, the school was renamed the US Coast Guard Academy when the Revenue Cutter Service was merged with the Life-Saving Service to become the US Coast Guard in 1915. The beautiful campus of the early academy was a major step up as a home for the cadets. (1940 *Tide Rips*.)

CADETS IN FORMATION AT FORT TRUMBULL. These cadets in formation are wearing traditional white sailor uniforms. The fort's buildings were dated and inappropriate for a modern university. When the Revenue Cutter School moved into the fort in 1910, the buildings were already 71 years old. (Courtesy of Public Affairs, Commandant US Coast Guard.)

THE ACADEMY UNDER CONSTRUCTION. This view looks north along what would become Campbell Street. The large building on the left is Satterlee Hall, named for Capt. Charles Satterlee (class of 1898). Satterlee was the commanding officer of the cutter *Tampa*, which was sunk by the German submarine *U-35* in World War I. (Courtesy of US Coast Guard Academy Facilities Engineering.)

WINTER OF 1942. The large building to the left is Chase Hall, where cadets lived. It is named for Salmon P. Chase, who served as secretary of the treasury and, later, as chief justice of the Supreme Court. The middle building (with the columns) is Hamilton Hall, the original home of the library and the administrative offices. The superintendent has his office here. The building to the right is Satterlee Hall, where classes are held. (1942 *Tide Rips*.)

CADETS HOLD COLORS IN FRONT OF HAMILTON HALL. This ceremony is performed every morning and evening. In addition to the national flag, the superintendent's flag is flown whenever he is in residence. The large flagpole was built as a replica of the mast on the cadet-training cutter *Alexander Hamilton*. (1933 *Tide Rips*.)

NEW LONDON SIGN. The city of New London proudly proclaims itself as the home of the US Coast Guard Academy. The academy has been in the New London area since 1910, when it was located at Fort Trumbull. It was moved to its current site in 1932. (1961 *Tide Rips*.)

CADETS MARCHING IN DOWNTOWN NEW LONDON, 1941. Classes graduated after three years during World War II. The academy expanded considerably during the war years. The Coast Guard was transferred into the US Navy during the war. The *Tide Rips* yearbooks during the war years accordingly had a picture of the Chief of Naval Operations as the service head of the Coast Guard. (1942 *Tide Rips*.)

OLDER BARRACKS, KNOWN AS "SPLINTER VILLAGE." The class of 1963 members in the Second Battalion lived in these relics from World War II. The Chase Hall expansion was completed in 1965. Since that time, all cadets have lived in Chase Hall. (Courtesy of Steve Ulmer.)

ACADEMY WATERFRONT SHOWING THE USCGC EAGLE. Jacobs Rock, home of the sailing activities of the academy, is a prominent spot. The Thames River is a beautiful location. The large Navy submarine base is located just upriver from the academy. During the author's four years at the academy, a cadet in one of the school's yachts made a submarine back down due to the rules of the road, which give right of way to sail over power. The cadet was subsequently given a class-one offense for embarrassing the submarine crew. (Courtesy of Steve Ulmer.)

CADETS PRACTICE SEMAPHORE ON WASHINGTON PARADE GROUND. The World War II years saw many changes at the academy. Not only were there changes to the curriculum, but many physical changes were also necessary to handle the large number of reserve officers passing through. (1942–1943 *Tide Rips.*)

THE ACADEMY IN THE 1950s. Note the absence of Roland Hall, Leamy Hall, the Alumni Center, and the press box for Jones Field. Smith Hall, the new library, and Dimick Hall were yet to be constructed. (Courtesy of US Coast Guard Academy Facilities Engineering.)

LOOKING NORTH TOWARD THE ACADEMY. In the center of this picture is the old fieldhouse, which was later torn down and replaced by the Alumni Center. The lower athletic practice fields have been greatly expanded since this photograph was taken. (Courtesy of US Coast Guard Academy Facilities Engineering.)

US Coast Guard Academy Alumni Center. The construction of the Alumni Center was funded by donations from alumni and sponsors. The third deck houses the Leadership Center and a boxing ring. (Author's collection.)

Ribbon-Cutting Ceremony at the Alumni Center, 2005. Handling the scissors is Rear Adm. Paul Busick (class of 1966), US Coast Guard (retired), who was the chair of the alumni association at the time of this ceremony. Paul had an older brother, Pete, who was a member of the class of 1963. Looking on is the superintendent of the academy, Rear Adm. Jim Van Sice (second from left; class of 1974). (Courtesy of the US Coast Guard Academy Alumni Association.)

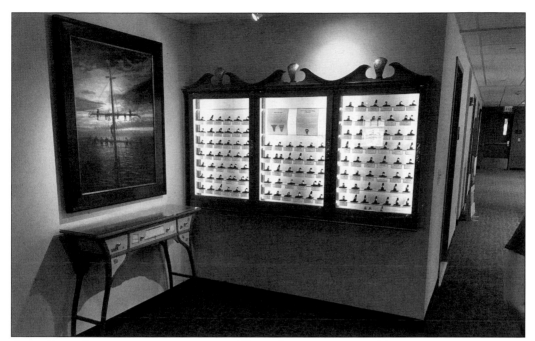

CLASS RING CABINET IN ALUMNI CENTER. This cabinet was created by Capt. Harvey Orr, US Coast Guard (retired). Captain Orr (class of 1963) also made the small table next to the cabinet. These items were alumni gifts nine and ten. At the time of the first gifts, which were given in 2005 and 2006, the then-president of the alumni association, Comdr. Jim Sylvester (class of 1971), said that Orr's creations were instrumental in "bringing our alumni center to life." Captain Orr was awarded the Distinguished Service Award from the US Coast Guard Academy Alumni Association in 2007. (Author's collection.)

THE ATHLETIC FIELDHOUSE. Indoor track and spring football practice were held here. Otto Graham would often demonstrate his passing ability by standing at one end of the basketball court in the building and throwing the football through the basket at the other end. This building was torn down to make room for the Alumni Center. (Courtesy of Steve Ulmer.)

A 1963 Class Ring in the Ring Display Cabinet. Cadets normally receive two rings. A miniature of the large ring is worn in the second-class year and replaced in the first-class year by the larger one, which the second class receives in April. Through the Golden Legacy Program sponsored by the alumni association, these rings are infused with the melted gold of class rings donated by alumni, connecting the Long Blue Line in a tangible way. This ring is a cadet's symbol of their alma mater and can be worn for the rest of his or her life. Each ring bears the academy crest on one side and the individual's class crest on the other. The class of 1963 had a controversial class crest, as it portrayed bare-chested mermaids holding a ship's helm. This ring worn by Rev. Steve Ulmer was gifted to the Alumni Center for it to be put on display. (Author's collection.)

BACK ENTRANCE OF SATTERLEE HALL.
This building was named after Capt.
Charles Satterlee (class of 1898), who
was the commanding officer of the
USCGC *Tampa*, which was sunk by
submarine torpedo on September
25, 1918, resulting in the loss of all
hands. The *Tampa* had just safely
escorted a convoy and was on its
way home. Located in Satterlee Hall
are the departments of leadership
and development, mathematics, and
humanities. (1940 *Tide Rips*.)

Satterlee Hall

**ACADEMY LIBRARY IN THE HENRIQUES
BUILDING.** The Henriques Building
was named for Capt. John Henriques,
who served at the Revenue Cutter
School of Instruction from 1876 to
1883. The murals on the walls were
painted as part of the Works Progress
Administration. The library was
later moved to its present location in
Waesche Hall. (1950 *Tide Rips*.)

COLOR GUARD PREPARES FOR A REVIEW OF CORPS OF CADETS ON WASHINGTON PARADE GROUND.
Reviews are frequently held on Saturday mornings before liberty is granted. They are
also held on special weekends, such as Parents' Weekend, Homecoming, and Graduation
Week, and whenever there is a distinguished visitor at the academy. (1952 *Tide Rips*.)

JACOBS ROCK. The home of the sailing center and the academy's competitive sailing program is on Jacobs Rock. More than 100 cadets participate in the program and its junior varsity sailing team. The academy has had several national champions, and the 2019 Bears offshore team finished second overall in the National Collegiate Large Yacht Championship for the John F. Kennedy Memorial Trophy. (Author's collection.)

CADET MARCHING BAND. The academy has an extensive music program, including two marching bands, a concert band, a pep band, a jazz band (the Nite-Caps), the Windjammer Drum and Bugle Corps, and singing groups (the Glee Club, Fair Winds, and Idlers). (1954 *Tide Rips.*)

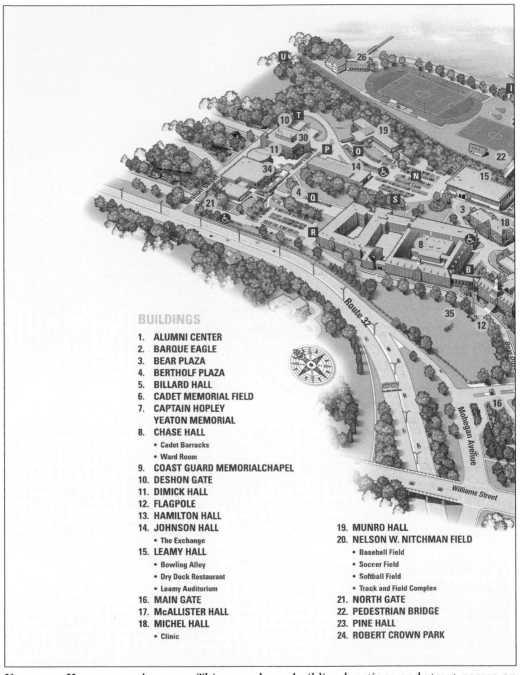

BUILDINGS

1. ALUMNI CENTER
2. BARQUE EAGLE
3. BEAR PLAZA
4. BERTHOLF PLAZA
5. BILLARD HALL
6. CADET MEMORIAL FIELD
7. CAPTAIN HOPLEY
   YEATON MEMORIAL
8. CHASE HALL
   • Cadet Barracks
   • Ward Room
9. COAST GUARD MEMORIALCHAPEL
10. DESHON GATE
11. DIMICK HALL
12. FLAGPOLE
13. HAMILTON HALL
14. JOHNSON HALL
    • The Exchange
15. LEAMY HALL
    • Bowling Alley
    • Dry Dock Restaurant
    • Leamy Auditorium
16. MAIN GATE
17. McALLISTER HALL
18. MICHEL HALL
    • Clinic

19. MUNRO HALL
20. NELSON W. NITCHMAN FIELD
    • Baseball Field
    • Soccer Field
    • Softball Field
    • Track and Field Complex
21. NORTH GATE
22. PEDESTRIAN BRIDGE
23. PINE HALL
24. ROBERT CROWN PARK

NORTHERN HALF OF THE ACADEMY. This map shows building locations and street names on the northern half of the campus. Building numbers are explained in the legend. (Courtesy of the US Coast Guard Academy Alumni Association.)

PARKING

HANDICAPPED PARKING

34. WAESCHE HALL
- Admissions
- Coast Guard Museum
- Library

35. WASHINGTON PARADE FIELD

36. YEATON HALL
- LDC

25. ROLAND HALL
26. ROWING CENTER / CREW
27. SAIL LOFT
28. SAILING CENTER / JACOB'S ROCK
29. SATTERLEE HALL
30. SMITH HALL
31. THE GUNS
32. THE HILL
33. THE OFFICERS CLUB

UNITED STATES
COAST GUARD
ACADEMY

New London, Connecticut
Telephone: 800-883-8724
Email: admission@uscga.edu | Web: www.uscga.edu
31 Mohegan Avenue | New London, CT 06320

SOUTHERN HALF OF THE ACADEMY. This map shows building locations and street names on the southern half of the campus. Building numbers are explained in the legend. (Courtesy of the US Coast Guard Academy Alumni Association.)

THE USCGC EAGLE. Built in Germany in 1936, the *Eagle* was a World War II war prize and became a part of the academy in 1946. Her length is 295 feet with a beam of 39 feet. The fore and main masts are 150 feet tall, and she carries 22 sails with a total of 21,350 square feet of canvas. The *Eagle* hosts 70,000 to 80,000 visitors each year. In 2018, the alumni association funded nearly $250,000 in improvements to the *Eagle*. (Author's collection.)

BASEBALL GAME. At this game held in the 1960s, the *Eagle* is moored in the background. The lower field has been renamed the Nelson W. Nitchman Field in honor of physical education instructor and coach "Nels" Nitchman, who was an assistant football coach at the academy from 1942 to 1945 and head coach from 1946 to 1958, when he was succeeded by Otto Graham. Nitchman also coached basketball at the academy from 1942 to 1954. (1966 *Tide Rips*.)

ACADEMY BOXING TEAM. Boxing was one of the earliest sports at the Revenue Cutter School of Instruction because it required little expensive equipment and taught self-defense. The sport was off and on over the years based on the periodic lack of a coach. In 2017, the academy boxing coach, Tom Barlie, was named the National Collegiate Boxing Association Coach of the Year. He left the academy in 2018 for another position, and the sport was shut down by the administration due to the lack of a coach and for safety reasons. (1940 *Tide Rips*.)

TRAINING BOATS (T-BOATS). T-Boats are used for ship-handling training. The boats are 65 years old and are named *Honor, Respect*, and *Duty*. The majority of cadet ship-handling training is done on the Ship Control and Navigation Training Systems (SCANTS) in Yeaton Hall. The ship simulators provide great experiences in ship-handling under various conditions, but there is something special about maneuvering an actual vessel and coordinating the actual docking of a ship. (Courtesy of the US Coast Guard Academy Alumni Association.)

WINTER SCENE, 1960s. This picture shows the old fieldhouse as well as the *Eagle* and Jacobs Rock on the waterfront. The *Eagle* is pictured without its distinctive speed stripe. The ship is no longer moored at the academy. (Courtesy of Steve Ulmer.)

CADET MEMORIAL CHAPEL. Located on the highest point at the academy, the chapel was built in 1952 thanks to donated funds. Incorporated in its design are symbols of the sacrifices of Coast Guard members, including the lectern dedicated to the memory of the USCGC *Escanaba*, which lost all but 2 of its 103 crew members in World War II. Attendance at religious services was mandatory during the four years the author attended the academy (from 1959 to 1963). The lighthouse beacon in the chapel steeple can be seen from great distances. (1959 *Tide Rips*.)

INTERIOR OF THE CHAPEL. The chapel was authorized by Congress on July 21, 1947, with the provision that it be funded by public subscription. A nationwide drive was launched in October 1948. The smallest donation was one cent, and the largest was $172,000, which was donated by the A.W. Mellon Educational and Charitable Trust; Mellon served as the secretary of the treasury from 1921 to 1932. The pews are made of solid mahogany and birch and can seat 480 people. (Author's collection.)

Three

PROCESS

The transition from high school to US Coast Guard commissioned officer is a complicated one, covering 200 weeks. It involves classroom studies and requires physical, intellectual, and professional values. Graduates must be capable of defending the nation and enforcing federal laws. The end result is the shaping of many diverse young men and women into a cohesive class with ties for a lifetime. The process is spread over four years, with the fourth class, or freshman, as follower. The sophomore, or third class, is the role model, with the second class, or junior, largely responsible for the hands-on shaping and operating of the corps. The seniors, or first class, are the overall leaders, setting and enforcing the mission. The Guide to Officer & Leader Development (GOLD) envisions a support team made up of an academic advisor, company officer/chief, port/activity coach, and mentors to produce leaders of character.

A portion of this evolution will be examined using two classes, the class that entered the academy in 1959 and the class that graduated in 2019. The period of 60 years between the two classes covers many changes in the academy that reflected priorities in society and the challenges the academy faces. During this period, the Coast Guard shifted from the Treasury Department to the Transportation Department and, finally, to the Department of Homeland Security. The makeup of the academy went from an all-male, nearly all-white corps of cadets to a diverse corps, one-third of which was female, with the highest percentage of underrepresented minorities of any military academy. The courses available to cadets expanded from a single track with only one major to multiple choices and nine different majors.

There have been significant improvements in selection using volunteer admission partners and a strong Academy Introductory Mission (AIM). The class that entered in 1959, with 181 taking the oath, commissioned 92, for an attrition rate of 50 percent. That class had only one underrepresented minority member—a Japanese American from Hawaii. The class of 2019 had 287 sworn in and graduated 240, for an attrition rate of 16 percent. That class had 101 females, 24 Asian Americans, 16 African Americans, and 13 people of Hispanic origin. The class of 1963 had graduates from 25 states and the District of Columbia. The class of 2019 contained graduates from 42 states and Washington, DC.

The military system remained in place for both of these classes. The first year is known as swab year. Swabs are required to follow rigid procedures when they are outside of their rooms. They have to be at attention with "eyes in the boat," meaning looking straight ahead. They stay in the center of all corridors, and all corners are "squared" (meaning that swabs must make a 90-degree turn). While going up and down "ladders" (stairs), swabs are to stay on the outside and square corners. When swabs are outside the academy buildings, they are required to march in formation. At meals, they sit on the forward three inches of their chairs, eyes in the boat, eating square meals and only speaking when addressed by an upperclassman. There is indoctrination information to be memorized for each day, and swabs are required to have a joke when asked. The swab year is a long year.

CADET SWABS OUT WITH RIFLES. Since the Coast Guard is a branch of the military, weapons training is required, although actual shooting is done during second-class summer (unless a cadet is on a rifle or pistol team). Today, training is done on M-16, 9-millimeter pistol, and shotgun. In 1961, the class of 1963 did small-arms training with the Marines at Quantico using M-1s and .45-caliber pistols. The Marine Corps and the Coast Guard have a close relationship that dates back to World War II, when Coast Guard coxswains manned the landing craft that put Marines on hostile shores. (1941 *Tide Rips*.)

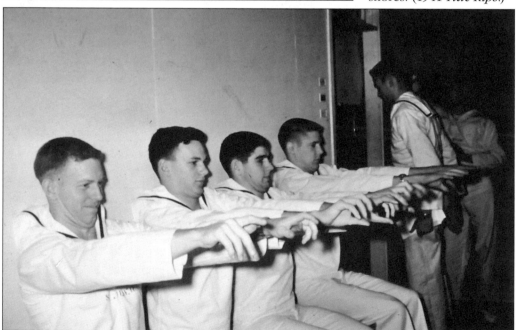

SWABS IN THE "GREEN BENCH." A particularly unpopular procedure was the green bench, so named for the sweat stain one left on the bulkhead. The swab year is monitored to avoid activities of a hazing nature that could be injurious. Behavior that has a racial or sexual element is strictly prohibited. (Courtesy of Steve Ulmer.)

CADETS IN QUADRANGLE. These cadets are doing exercises with the M-1 rifle. "Butts and Muzzles" is hard work but teaches military skills. The M-1 weighed just under 10 pounds, and it required considerable arm strength and endurance to do this exercise for any length of time. (1947 *Tide Rips*.)

ACADEMY INTRODUCTORY MISSION (AIM) OATH. The AIM program, which began in 1966, is an improvement to the selection process. Here, prospective cadets between their junior and senior years of high school attend a week of extensive training at the academy. The successful completion of AIM is a good indicator of future success at the academy. The rising members of the class of 2019 included 37 percent who were AIM graduates. There was no AIM program in place for the class of 1963. (Author's collection.)

ACADEMY INTRODUCTORY MISSION (AIM) PARTICIPANTS MARCHING. Participants learn the basics of military discipline over a one-week period. The program is realistic and gives the prospective cadets a feel for swab year. Approximately 300 high school students participate in AIM during the summer before their senior year, and the academy offers three weeklong sessions. (Author's collection.)

ACADEMY INTRODUCTORY MISSION (AIM) PARTICIPANTS AT THE WATERFRONT. Here, AIMers enjoy waterfront fun as they try their hands at sailing at Jacobs Rock. Those who successfully complete the AIM week are much more likely to adapt to life at the academy, which has helped to reduce the attrition rate. In the case of the class of 1963, the rate of attrition was over 50 percent. (Author's collection.)

ACADEMY INTRODUCTORY MISSION (AIM) COMPETITION. Teams demonstrate their teamwork by constructing and operating a radio-controlled boat to accomplish a number of Coast Guard missions, including placing a buoy, rescuing survivors from the water, ice-breaking, cleaning up pollution, and others. It is truly amazing how this diverse group of high school juniors develops into cohesive teams in such a short time. (Author's collection.)

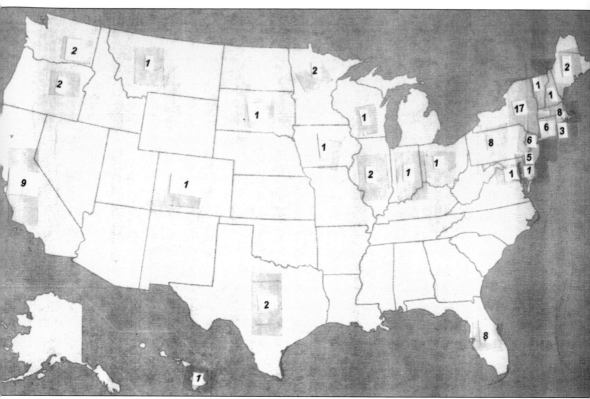

MAP OF 1963 GRADUATES. This map made by the author shows the home states of the graduates of the US Coast Guard Academy class of 1963. Northeastern states provided 46 of the 93 graduates. Only Florida, with 8 graduates, represented the Southeast. Fourteen members came from the West, and nine came from the Great Lakes. New York was the source of the most graduates—17. Twenty-two states had no graduates in the class of 1963. (Author's collection.)

THE ACADEMY REGULATIONS. These were the laws cadets lived by. Infractions led to demerits and determined how much liberty a cadet could have. More than 25 demerits in a month meant no liberty the following month. Demerits also factored into class standing. (1961 *Tide Rips*.)

CHAIN GANG. An innovation that started with the class of 2011 was linking the inbound class with the class that would have its 50th anniversary during the year of that class's graduation. The members of the class of 1963 and their spouses assembled for the reporting-in day of the class of 2013. Throughout the four years of the class of 2013, members of the class of 1963 would attend their special events. It was especially helpful for the parents of the incoming class to have some reassurance at reporting-in day that their sons and daughters were joining a special group—known as the Long Blue Line— that would care for them. (Author's collection.)

THE HONOR WALK. At the end of their seven-week Swab Summer, the members of the class of 2013 were taken on a special event called the Honor Walk. Led by the second-class cadets, the walk is held in the evening in the Robert Crown Park adjacent to the Memorial Chapel. Members of the fourth class are led through a series of dramas played in costume by second-class cadets depicting events in Coast Guard history. The event ends at the tomb of Hopley Yeaton, the first commissioned officer of the Revenue Cutter Service. (Author's collection.)

CLASS OF 2013 ARRIVING AT CROWN PARK FOR THE HONOR WALK. King Neptune led the group. The atmosphere of the Robert Crown Park at dusk provides a dramatic setting for the events that are presented in the hour-long process. (Author's collection.)

THE 1940 CORPS. Cadets stand proudly in formation in the early days at the New London campus. The modern cadets are organized as one regiment divided into eight companies, each of which is composed of about 120 cadets of all classes. The highest-ranking cadet in each company is the company commander. At the top of the cadet chain of command is the regimental commander, the highest-ranking cadet. Command positions, both in companies and on regimental staff, are highly competitive, and a cadet's overall class rank is often a deciding factor in who is awarded the position. The eight companies are named for the first eight letters of the NATO phonetic alphabet. Each has a special focus in the administration of day-to-day affairs. Alpha Company manages health and wellness. Bravo Company runs training. Charlie Company administers the honor system. Delta Company coordinates drills and ceremonies. Echo Company manages transportation and logistics. Foxtrot Company operates the cadet conduct system, organizes the watch rotations, and updates cadet regulations. Golf Company is in charge of cleaning supplies and repairing damaged rooms within Chase Hall. Hotel Company is in charge of morale events. To accomplish these missions, each company is divided, along shipboard lines, into three departments, each of which is divided into divisions with specific responsibilities. Divisions are the most basic unit at the Coast Guard Academy, and each has a very specific purpose. Each division is led by a first-class cadet and contains several members of each other class. (1940 *Tide Rips*.)

AERIAL VIEW OF THE COAST GUARD ACADEMY. The academy campus and surroundings are captured in this picture. The campus encompasses over 100 acres both purchased and donated by the City of New London. Jean Hamlet, daughter of academy superintendent Rear Adm. Harry G. Hamlet, broke ground on the campus in January 1931. The cornerstone for Hamilton Hall was laid by Secretary of the Treasury Andrew W. Mellon in May 1931. (Courtesy of Coast Guard Academy Facilities Engineering.)

COMBAT INFORMATION CENTER (CIC). Cadets work in a CIC on a summerlong cruise. For all classes, the summerlong cruises on the *Eagle* are significant events during training. The long cruise for the class of 1963, held at the start of third-class year in 1960, went from New London to Portsmouth, England; Oslo, Norway; and Le Havre, France. Cadets sailed on the *Eagle*, with the cutters *Absecon* and *Yakutat* making up the squadron. In 1962, at the start of the cadets' first-class year, the cruise went from the academy to Edinburgh, Scotland; Antwerp, Belgium; and Las Palmas, Spain. (1963 *Tide Rips*.)

WORKING ON THE *EAGLE'S* STERN. Cruising on the *Eagle* and the accompanying cutters is not all fun and games. The *Eagle* is over 80 years old and requires daily maintenance of her wooden decks and paint to protect her from the maritime environment. (1950 *Tide Rips*.)

ON WATCH. The *Eagle* has an engine room where cadets stand evaporator watch. These members of the class of 1963 are Jim Webster (left), who later became an aviator and aviation-engineering officer, and Joe Hughes, who was tragically killed in an automobile accident en route to his first duty station. (1963 *Tide Rips*.)

CONNECTICUT WINTER. The New London weather is not always friendly, especially for cadets from Florida and California. Winters in New London are cold. Fortunately for the class of 1963, they never went through a hurricane during their four years at the academy. (1954 *Tide Rips*.)

SNOWBALL FIGHT. The secret to New England weather is to enjoy what one gets. This image shows a snowball fight by the observatory. The long topcoat, known as a bridge coat, was a welcome piece of apparel in the cadet wardrobe. Unfortunately, the combination hat was not designed for warmth. (1951 *Tide Rips*.)

SUPREME COURT JUSTICE ANTONIN SCALIA VISITS THE ACADEMY. Justice Scalia was appointed by Pres. Ronald Reagan and served from 1986 until his death in 2016. Throughout the cadets' 200 weeks at the academy, distinguished leaders from the government and the military are invited to make a visit to address cadets. Often, a review is held in their honor. (Courtesy of US Coast Guard Academy petty officer third class Cory Mendenhall.)

HH-65 HELICOPTER. The summer program at the start of second-class year includes an introduction to Coast Guard Aviation known as Cadet Aviation Training Unit (CATU). For the class of 1963, CATU was held at Elizabeth City Air Station in North Carolina. Later classes did CATU at the Aviation Training Center in Mobile, Alabama. Beginning in 1984, flights at CATU in Mobile were made in the then-new HH-65A. The HH-65 replaced the HH-52A Sikorsky helicopter, which saved more lives than any other helicopter. The 99 HH-52s flown by the Coast Guard are now retired. (Author's collection.)

HOIST TRAINING. Approximately 10 to 20 percent of each class will attend flight training in Pensacola, Florida, and Corpus Christi, Texas, with the US Navy. Additional obligated service is required for those who attend postgraduate training such as flight training. The Coast Guard has a higher percentage of aviators in the officer ranks than any other service. Here, an HH-65 practices a boat hoist with a Coast Guard small boat from Station New London. (Courtesy of Coast Guard Academy Public Affairs, Zach Kayser.)

RED BIRD AVIATION SIMULATOR. Simulator administrator cadet third class Jackson Carpenter stands in front of the Red Bird Aviation Simulator in Chase Hall. The $105,000 simulator was a gift from the class of 1949 and the alumni association. It has significantly added to the aviation experience opportunity for cadets. (Courtesy of the US Coast Guard Academy Alumni Association.)

HUMAN PYRAMID. The process has its high points in first-class year. Here, the leaders of Foxtrot Company enjoy some time together. Of note are the three on the far left of the bottom row—from left to right, Jim Webster, Gerry Woolever, and Dave Zwick—who graduated as the top three members of the class of 1963. Harry Suzuki (farthest right in the second row) was the single Asian American and minority in the class. (1963 *Tide Rips*.)

RING DANCE. A traditional highlight is the Ring Dance, held at the end of second-class year before the long cruise. This is when many of the class become engaged, often giving their intended the miniature ring worn throughout second-class year as an engagement ring. Cadets are required to attend at least two formal dances each year. (1954 *Tide Rips*.)

USCGC *ABSECON* (WAVP-374). The long cruise usually lasts for 10 weeks. Cadets split their time between the *Eagle* and the two accompanying high-endurance cutters. It is a time to take many star fixes with the sextant and use the theory learned in the classroom. The liberty in European and other ports is definitely a plus. Note the absence of the distinctive red and blue "speed stripe" found on modern Coast Guard cutters. (1963 *Tide Rips*.)

ROPE WORK. Time aboard the *Eagle* gives cadets an opportunity to experience the traditions of life aboard ships in the days of sail. It teaches an appreciation for the importance of paying attention to the weather and the hard work required to keep the ship and its rigging in shape. The author, who came from the desert region of Washington State, had his only seagoing experience on the Columbia River prior to his time in the Coast Guard. Climbing the rigging on the high seas was a meaningful indoctrination into these traditions. (1954 *Tide Rips*.)

CADET FIRST CLASS JACKSON KALAMA. Kalama, shown here in 2016, was a foreign exchange student from Rwanda. Up to 36 members of the US Coast Guard Academy can be foreign exchange students. The program fosters universal understanding between different countries. Strong lifetime bonds develop between class members. (Courtesy of US Coast Guard Academy Public Affairs.)

SANDHURST TEAM, 2017. The Coast Guard Academy team has competed in the Sandhurst competition at the Military Academy at West Point. Sandhurst is the world's premier international military skills competition. It consists of a two-day course involving 13 day and night events. In the 2017 competition, the US Coast Guard Academy team defeated 29 of 38 West Point teams and the Naval Academy team. (Courtesy of Paul Duddy.)

CLASS OF 1963 BRAVO COMPANY. The four-class system of learners, watchers, trainers, and leaders has its desired result of creating close bonds among its members. Members of the group have to help one another to successfully meet their challenges. These bonds remain throughout the members' active duty careers and into the remainder of their civilian careers and retirement. (1963 *Tide Rips*.)

Four

PEOPLE

Academy graduates join the Long Blue Line, meaning there is a significant history associated with academy personnel. However, graduates are only a percentage of the total Coast Guard personnel who have worn the uniform and contributed the Coast Guard's accomplishments. The Long Blue Line started in 1790, when Alexander Hamilton, with the support of Pres. George Washington, started the Revenue Cutter Service. The academy joined the line in 1876, when the Revenue Cutter School of Instruction was started on the *Dobbin*. The author selected the following men and women because they represent a particular event of significance or made a singular contribution to Coast Guard history.

The academy is rich with people of significance. Many of the buildings on campus are named for individuals who had an impact on the academy or the service. Some were faculty members, like professor Chester E. Dimick, who headed the mathematics department from 1906 to 1945; Capt. Charles A. McAllister, who was engineer in chief for the Coast Guard from 1905 to 1919; and Rear Adm. Edward H. "Iceberg" Smith (class of 1913), who was a legendary Arctic expert. Some buildings were named after athletic standouts like Nelson W. Nitchman, who was the coach of the academy football and basketball teams, and Capt. Otto Graham, who was a football coach and athletic director at the academy. Others were superintendents, like Rear Adm. Frank Leamy (class of 1925), who was superintendent from 1957 to 1961, or commandants like Ellsworth P. Berthoff (class of 1889), the first commandant of the modern day Coast Guard and the namesake of Berthoff Plaza, and World War II commandant Adm. Russell R. Waesche (class of 1906). One building is named for the only Coast Guard Medal of Honor recipient, PO1 Douglas Albert Munro.

The list is not exclusive and was selected by the author because of its importance to the overall history or because of the individual's unique contribution. The overland rescue principals included two graduates driving dog sleds and herding reindeer in the Arctic to save hundreds of people who were starving. One was a commandant who held the office for 10 years. There are many "firsts" among the selectees. Included is the first Asian American graduate, the first African American graduate, the first female graduate to make flag rank, the first female regimental commander, the first African American female regimental commander, and the first astronaut from the Coast Guard. There are those who set records or were champions. All of them have brought credit to the Coast Guard.

ALEXANDER HAMILTON. Alexander Hamilton was the first secretary of the treasury and the creator of the Revenue Cutter Service, or Revenue Marine. At only 33 years of age, Hamilton was a close advisor to Pres. George Washington and a brilliant soldier and politician. In 2018, this sculpture of Alexander Hamilton was dedicated and donated to the academy by the class of 1963. (Author's collection.)

THE THREE PRINCIPALS IN THE OVERLAND EXPEDITION. Incredibly, these men traveled 1,500 miles in 100 days during the arctic winter of 1897–1898 driving dog sleds with supplies and more than 300 reindeer to whalers who had become trapped in ice. First Lt. David Jarvis (right; class of 1883), was the leader. Second Lt. Ellsworth Berthoff (left; class of 1889) later became commandant. The surgeon, Dr. Samuel Call, was not an academy graduate. All three were awarded Congressional Gold Medals for the daring rescue. (Courtesy of US Coast Guard District 17 Public Affairs.)

METAL CUP ENGRAVED WITH 1ST LT. DAVID JARVIS'S NAME. The metal cup used by Jarvis during the Overland Expedition rescue is in the US Coast Guard Academy Museum. This amazing rescue was unique for the Coast Guard and involved traveling nearly 1,500 miles in the Alaskan winter, much of it above the Arctic Circle in darkness—not usual sailor skills. (Author's collection.)

VICE ADM. HARRY G. HAMLET (CLASS OF 1896). Hamlet was superintendent of the US Coast Guard Academy from 1928 to 1932 and, later, the seventh commandant of the Coast Guard. He served with distinction with the Navy during World War I. Only two years after he was commissioned, he was assigned to the R/C *Bear* during the Overland Expedition. The 1934 *Tide Rips* was dedicated to Hamlet. (1934 *Tide Rips*.)

ADM. RUSSELL R. WAESCHE (CLASS OF 1906), EIGHTH COMMANDANT. Waesche was commandant of the Coast Guard for 10 years, from 1936 to 1946. He led the Coast Guard throughout World War II, when the service grew nearly tenfold to 214,000. In 2019, the Coast Guard had 40,992 active-duty and 7,000 reserve members. (1940 *Tide Rips*.)

Admiral Russell R. Waesche

COMMANDANT, UNITED STATES COAST GUARD

Lt. Jack Ngum Jones (Class of 1949). Jones was the first Asian American graduate of the US Coast Guard Academy. He graduated from the California Institute of Technology in 1945 prior to attending the academy. He was captain of the baseball team during his first-class year. His service career included working in communications management and law. (1949 *Tide Rips*.)

Comdr. Meryl James Smith Jr. (Class of 1966). Smith was the first African American graduate of the academy. He earned a Bronze Star for duties in Vietnam, where he was the first African American to command a US warship in close combat. He graduated from George Washington University Law School and became a staff lawyer for General Dynamic Electric Boat in Groton following his Coast Guard career. This portrait is in Hamilton Hall. (Author's collection.)

BUST OF OTTO GRAHAM. This bust is centrally located on the stage of the Otto Graham Center for Athletic Excellence in Billard Hall. Captain Graham coached academy football for nine seasons, including the undefeated 1963 team. He also served as head of athletics for 22 years. (Author's collection.)

SUPERINTENDENT REAR ADM. STEPHEN HADLEY EVANS (CLASS OF 1927) PRESENTS RECOGNITION TO CDR. OTTO GRAHAM. Graham (left) received a certificate from Superintendent Evans for being inducted into the College Football Hall of Fame in 1956. Graham earned All-American honors in both football and basketball and placed third in the Heisman Trophy competition during his senior year at Northwestern University in 1943. (Courtesy of US Coast Guard Academy Museum.)

Commander Graham receives his College Football Hall of Fame certificate from the U.S. Coast Guard Academy Superintendent Rear Admiral Stephen Evans

BRUCE EDWARD MELNICK. Astronaut Bruce Edward Melnick (left; class of 1972) is pictured with the author at the Elizabeth City Coast Guard Aviation Pterodactyl Roost in 2009. Melnick retired as a commander from the Coast Guard. In 1975, he earned a master of science degree from the University of West Florida. He earned a Defense Superior Service Medal, a Defense Distinguished Service Medal, and a NASA Flight Medal. He is a retired astronaut. (Author's collection.)

PAINTING OF M/V PRINSENDAM RESCUE. This ship was on fire and adrift in the Gulf of Alaska in October 1980. This painting is in the foyer of the Alumni Center. When Bruce Melnick was stationed at the Sitka Coast Guard Air Station, he took part in the successful rescue of the 519 passengers and crew. At the time, this was considered the most successful rescue ever, with no serious injuries. He was awarded a Distinguished Flying Cross for hoisting over 100 passengers. (Author's collection.)

REAR ADM. SANDRA STOSZ (1982). Stosz was the first female to serve as the head of a US military academy. She was also the first female graduate of the Coast Guard Academy to be selected for flag rank. (Author's collection.)

HALL OF HEROES PRESENTATION. Rear Adm. Sandra Stosz is shown presenting a Hall of Heroes plaque to Capt. Dave Andrews, US Coast Guard (retired), class of 1963. The induction ceremony was held on November 7, 2014. Captain Andrews was recognized with a Distinguished Flying Cross in 1973 for saving two lives in heavy weather near San Clemente Island in California. The Distinguished Flying Cross had been presented to then lieutenant commander Andrews personally by Secretary of Transportation Samuel Skinner. (Courtesy of Lorna Andrews.)

CADET FIRST CLASS LINDA JOHANSEN (1980).
The military program of the academy reached a milestone when Cadet First Class Linda Johansen became the first woman to lead the corps of cadets at any military academy. Women can hold any job in the Coast Guard. In the class of 2019, 100 of the 230 graduates were women. In 2020, Adm. Thad Allen, the 23rd commandant, stated at an academy assembly that the smartest thing the Coast Guard had ever done was accepting women into the academy. (1980 *Tide Rips*.)

CLASS OF 1944 MARCHING TO GRADUATION.
All of the classes of World War II were heroes. Note that their uniforms are still marked as cadets second class, as they are graduating one year early. There were 83 graduates in this class. In 1945, there were 105 graduates. In 1946, there were 107 new ensigns. The numbers peaked in 1947 with 127. Reflecting the end of the war, there were only 58 graduates in 1948. (1944 *Tide Rips*.)

ADM. THAD WILLIAM ALLEN (CLASS OF 1971), 23RD COMMANDANT. Pres. George W. Bush designated Allen as principal federal officer for Hurricane Katrina, and Pres. Barack Obama named him a national incident commander for the Deepwater Horizon oil spill. Allen was the son of a Coast Guard chief petty officer. In 2002, at the Dining In, a formal dinner with historical military traditions, when Allen was the guest of honor, he brought a pair of his father's uniform shoes and dedicated his talk to "Big Shoes to Fill." (Courtesy of US Coast Guard.)

FRED FURAUS (CLASS OF 1963) AND DAVID R. ZWICK (CLASS OF 1963). Furaus (left) and Zwick are pictured in Vietnam. Following his obligated service, Zwick attended Harvard Law School, during which time he joined Ralph Nader's "Nader's Raiders." He founded the Clear Water Action organization, coauthored *The Water Wasteland* with Marcy Benstock, and helped to write and secure passage of the Clean Water Act of 1972. Zwick graduated from Harvard Law School and also earned a master's degree in public policy from the John F. Kennedy School of Government. (Courtesy of Jim Furaus.)

CADET FIRST CLASS NAISSE PIERRE (CLASS OF 2020). Pierre is a resident of Haiti and is the first international cadet to serve as regimental commander. The special category of international cadets may have up to 36 enrolled at any one time. These cadets apply for admission through the defense attaché office of their country's US embassy. (Courtesy of Paul Duddy.)

ADM. EDWIN J. ROLAND (CLASS OF 1929), 12TH COMMANDANT. Roland's class graduated 30 members. He was captain of the 1931 football team that defeated the Marines, Army, and Navy to win the President's Cup. He was also captain of the basketball team in his senior year. During World War II, he was chief of enlisted personnel, and he was later commander of an escort division. He was the plank owner as the first commanding officer of the icebreaker *Mackinaw* (WAGB-83). Selected for a flag on July 1, 1956, he first commanded the First District in Boston and was later commander of the Eastern Area and Third District in New York. He was appointed commandant on April 23, 1962, and during his watch, he assigned 82-foot Coast Guard patrol boats to Vietnam. He taught physics and mathematics at the academy. He was the first inductee into the Academy Athletic Hall of Fame. (1939 *Tide Rips*.)

PO1 Douglas Munro. This portrait hangs in the lobby of the US Coast Guard Academy barracks named in Munro's honor. He was awarded the Medal of Honor for action he took during the Battle of Guadalcanal on September 27, 1942, when he used his Higgins boat to cover the successful evacuation of a company of Marines who were threatened to be overrun by Japanese soldiers. He was 22 years old when he died from his wounds. Munro is the only non-Marine enshrined in the Wall of Heroes of the National Museum of the Marine Corps. (Author's collection.)

Five

PROGRAMS

The academy mission is to graduate young men and women well-grounded in seamanship, science, and the humanities. To do this requires a rigorous schedule of courses and activities. The dean of academics, Kurt J. Colella, PhD, PE, states:

> The US Coast Guard Academy is a place that offers a four-year experience filled with exciting challenges that foster the intellectual, physical, and professional growth of our future Coast Guard leadership. With a student-to-faculty ratio of approximately eight-to-one, our mantra is to develop a professional relationship with each and every cadet that supports their development and unlocks their potential.

US News & World Report, the *Princeton Review*, and *Forbes* magazine recognize the US Coast Guard Academy as one of the top institutions of higher learning in the country.

The original School of Instruction of the Revenue Cutter Service started in 1876 with eight cadets and three instructors on the R/C *Dobbin*. When it began, the course of instruction was two years with an emphasis on ship-handling. Engineering was not stressed, as the intention was to obtain ship engineers from outside sources. The course of instruction was extended to three years in 1903.

The academy moved to its current location from Fort Trumbull in 1932. It was accredited by the Association of American Universities in 1940 and was given the authority to grant bachelor of science degrees. In 1946, the barque *Eagle*, a prize of war, was commissioned into the US Coast Guard.

For the class of 1963, there was a single track. Everyone took the same courses for all four years and was awarded a bachelor of science degree in engineering upon graduation. For the class of 2019, there was much more opportunity for cadets to choose a major that aligns with their particular interests and abilities. The academy now offers nine majors: civil engineering, electrical engineering, mechanical engineering, naval architecture and marine engineering, government, management, operations research, cybersecurity, and computer analysis.

In addition to the educational program, which is typical for any university, the academy has a professional curriculum and physical program that is not so typical at nonmilitary colleges. The summer program held during each cadet year introduces more things that must be mastered with hands-on training on the ocean and at operational units. The athletic program has its own chapter in "Play."

THE NEW ACADEMY FROM THE RIVER

Curriculum of the New Academy

FOURTH CLASS

First Semester

Seamanship
Communications
Chemistry
Algebra
Trigonometry
English
French
Physical Education
Shop
Chemistry Laboratory
Drills

Second Semester

Seamanship
Astronomy
Communications
Chemistry
Algebra
Trigonometry
Descriptive Geometry
English
French
Physical Education
Drawing
Shop
Chemistry Laboratory
Drills

THIRD CLASS

First Semester

Seamanship
Navigation
Communications
Calculus
Physics
English
French
Heat Engines
Physical Education
Drawing
Physics Laboratory
Drills

Second Semester

Seamanship
Navigation Law
Navigation
Communications
Mechanics
English
French
Heat Engines
Physical Education
Drawing
Engineering Laboratory
Drills

CURRICULUM OF THE ACADEMY, 1933. The classes for this year were similar to those taken by the class of 1963 in its first year, 1959. They included chemistry, algebra, trigonometry, English composition, communication, practical seamanship, graphics, analytical geometry, calculus, basic machines, and physical education. (1933 *Tide Rips*.)

Physics Class. In this picture, professor Cdr. Rod White (center; class of 1950) is teaching cadets third class Dave Zwick (left; class of 1963) and Dana Starkweather (class of 1963) about physics. Other courses taken in the third-class year included analytical geometry, calculus, modern world history, seamanship, navigation, US foreign policy, meteorology, and physical education. (1959 *Tide Rips.*)

SAILING ON THE THAMES. The waterfront program is extensive, involving 120 vessels, and covers everything from basic seamanship and knot-tying to competitive sailing at the national level. The academy mission requires a liking for the sea and its lore. Academy graduates have a reputation of familiarity with the sea. (1967 *Tide Rips*.)

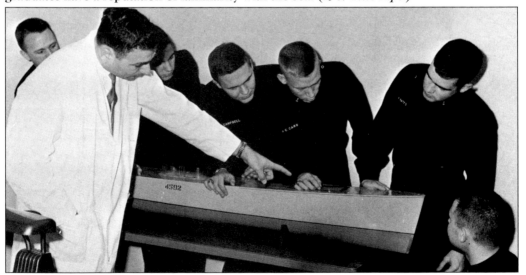

NAVAL ARCHITECTURE. Ship design is an important part of the academic program. For the class of 1963, this was the highest-weighted subject during the senior (or first-class) year. Oversight of the merchant marine industry and the safe operation of the nation's ports require knowledge of ship design, construction, and operation. (1964 *Tide Rips*.)

EARLY SIKORSKY HELICOPTER. This extremely basic helicopter was flown to the Washington Parade Ground from Floyd Bennett Field in Brooklyn. This would have been a flight requiring some daring given the distance and lack of navigational facilities. The pilot was the legendary "Stu" Graham. (1947 *Tide Rips*.)

AVIATION INDOCTRINATION. Cadets spend time with a PBY aircraft at Elizabeth City Air Station in the 1940s. The aviation familiarity program has always been popular with cadets. In the case of the class of 1963, part of the training involved a flight from Elizabeth City, North Carolina, to Miami. (1948 *Tide Rips*.)

HEADING TO FORMATION. Cadets proceed to formation in wartime gray uniforms. The Coast Guard was the first service to wear the wartime gray uniform. World War II ushered in a major emphasis on the military program at the academy. These uniforms are no longer in use. (1942–1943 *Tide Rips*.)

WAR IS DECLARED, DECEMBER 8, 1941.
Cadets listen to Pres. Franklin D.
Roosevelt's "Day of Infamy" speech. The
Coast Guard had been transferred into
the Navy on November 1, 1941. These
cadets knew that they were destined to
see action upon graduation. (1942–1943
Tide Rips.)

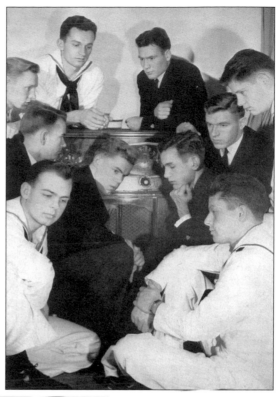

**CADETS MAN A MACHINE
GUN.** The academy's
Charlie Company was
responsible for machine
guns and mortars. As
World War II escalated,
training at the academy
was changed to include
more defense-related
items. The Coast Guard
would participate in
nearly every theater in the
war. (1938 *Tide Rips*.)

INSIDE THE CHAPEL. The religious program for the cadets centers around the US Coast Guard Memorial Chapel. There are both Protestant and Catholic choirs. The chapel is busy after graduation as cadets, who are forbidden to marry while they are at the academy, make up for lost time. (1950 *Tide Rips*.)

THE US COAST GUARD MEMORIAL CHAPEL. The chapel had been incorporated in the original plans for the academy, but the use of public funds to construct a chapel had caused much discussion. It was not until 1947 that Congress authorized the Coast Guard to build the chapel, but the funds needed to be raised through public subscription. A nationwide drive commenced. The largest contribution was $172,000 (from the A.W. Mellon Educational and Charitable Trust). Andrew W. Mellon was the secretary of the treasury from 1921 to 1932 and had always had a keen interest in the Coast Guard. (Author's collection.)

THE ACADEMY MEMORIAL CHAPEL INTERIOR. The pews provide seating for 480 and are made of solid mahogany and birch. The suspended lamps are designed in the motif of old whale-oil lamps. The organ is a three-manual digital electronic Renaissance model and was a gift from the class of 1950 given at the time of their 50th reunion. The lectern is dedicated to the 101 crew members of the USCGC *Escanaba*, which was lost at sea in World War II. (Author's collection.)

ARCH OF SWORDS. A traditional military wedding requires six officers to form an arch of swords for the newlyweds. This was a windfall for those classmates who were not getting married, as they were invited to weddings across the country. The author went to six: Katz, a Jewish wedding at Idlewild Airport; Bluett in Baltimore; Heller in Grand Junction, Colorado; North in San Marino, California; Andrews in Long Beach; and Shorey in Pensacola, Florida. (1947 *Tide Rips*.)

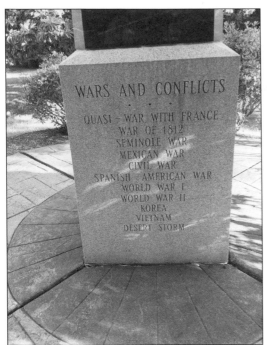

ENGRAVING ON THE WARS AND CONFLICTS MONUMENT. This monument is situated adjacent to the chapel in Robert Crown Park, which contains a number of historic and significant memorials. This black granite monument records all of the national conflicts in which the Coast Guard has participated. In the Quasi-War with France, the service was the only seagoing force, as the Navy had been disestablished. Pres. Barack Obama commented during his remarks at the 2015 graduation that he had seen Coast Guard personnel in the audience when he visited Afghanistan, which was a long way from the ocean. (Author's collection.)

BATTLE STREAMERS OF THE COAST GUARD. Each streamer represents a battle or conflict in which the Coast Guard or Revenue Marine participated. This display is in the Coast Guard wing of the National Naval Aviation Museum in Pensacola, Florida. (Author's collection.)

COLUMBARIUM. This is the only official Coast Guard burial site, which was dedicated on October 17, 2014. It is adjacent to the memorial chapel in the Robert Crown Park. The ashes of deceased service members and their wives can be placed here. The columbarium was built with donated funds. (Author's collection.)

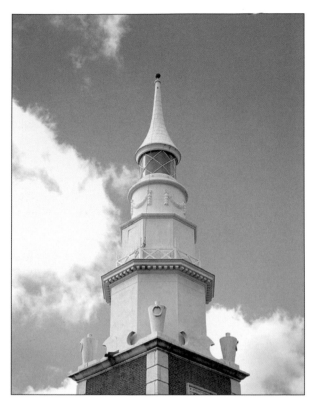

CHAPEL LIGHTHOUSE SPIRE. The chapel lantern is a typical pierhead tower lantern like those in common use on the Great Lakes. Below the light is the widow's walk, added in memory of the wives of seafaring men who looked seaward in a vigil for their sailors coming home. This light can be seen from a great distance throughout the New London area. (Author's collection.)

ORIGINAL POSITION OF THE MAIN GATE. This road leads up the hill toward the superintendent's quarters and other senior staff quarters and ends at the chapel. The Robert Crown Park is behind the chapel. (1940 *Tide Rips*.)

LONG CRUISE, 1931. The summer program's long cruises are very popular and a unique part of the academy experience. This particular cruise covered 10,000 miles and included stops in Gibraltar, Egypt, Turkey, France, and the Canary Islands. In the early years, before the Revenue Cutter School of Instruction came ashore, these cruises could last for up to six months. (1932 *Tide Rips*.)

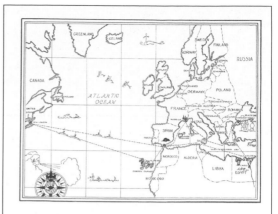

Cruise of 1931

PORTS OF CALL

PARRIS ISLAND, S. C.

GIBRALTAR, B. P.

ALEXANDRIA, EGYPT

Cairo, Egypt

CONSTANTINOPLE, TURKEY

MARSEILLES, FRANCE

LAS PALMAS, CANARY ISLANDS

10,000 Miles

PICTURES FROM THE 1931 CRUISE. Some members of this group of cadets are sitting on camels with the iconic Egyptian pyramids in the background. The Sphinx is immediately behind the cadets. This famous structure with the body of a lion and head of a person is thought to have been built around 2494 BC. It was long believed that Napoleon's artillery damaged the structure, but that claim has since been disputed. (1932 *Tide Rips*.)

CRUISE TO BRUSSELS, 1960. These cadets are shown at an open-air market in Oslo, Norway. This was a particularly popular liberty stop. The beautiful Frogner Park, with its amazing statues, was impressive. The people were also quite welcoming. (Courtesy of Steve Ulmer.)

R/C SALMON P. CHASE. This was the primary training vessel for the academy from 1878 to 1907. She was a 115-foot barque-rigged clipper. The ship was named for Lincoln's secretary of the treasury, Salmon P. Chase. She was homeported at the north end of Fish Island in New Bedford, Massachusetts, and later moved to Curtis Bay, Maryland. In 1895, the *Chase* was cut in two, and 40 feet were added to make more room for cadets. Most classes were small during this period, with numbers of graduates in the single digits. Ten graduated in 1896, one of whom was Harry Hamlet, who later served as superintendent and vice admiral. (Courtesy of US Coast Guard Commandant Public Relations.)

F O R E W O R D

ENVIRONMENTAL CREATURES are able to survive only by virtue of a constant process of adaptation to their surroundings. We of the Corps have learned to break up the monotony of our regimented lives with stolen moments of boisterousness, and to relieve the tedious, boring aspects of our training with a penetrating and understanding insight into the problems, sorrows, and joys of our classmates. The rugged and enduring friendships which a Cadet forms while at the Academy are his most priceless possessions. This book will attempt to bring these friends somewhat closer at times when he most needs their unquestioning loyalty and solid support.

FOREWORD FROM THE 1939 *TIDE RIPS*. These sentiments—written nearly a century ago for the 25 graduates of the class of 1939—were relevant to the author's class of 1963 and are still so today. The development of class spirit is evident in the high percentage of graduates who return for homecomings. (1939 *Tide Rips*.)

SAILING SHIP *DANMARK*. This Danish training vessel was in US waters when the Nazis overran Denmark. The captain placed his ship and crew at the disposal of the US government. The ship was built in 1933 and was 252 feet long. She was a full-rigged sailing ship and was used in the training of more than 3,000 cadets and reserve officer candidates during the war years from 1942 to 1945. The vessel returned home to Denmark and is still in use today. (Courtesy of US Coast Guard Commandant Public Relations.)

BOAT DRILLS ON A LONG CRUISE. Cadets spent an extensive number of days at sea during a long cruise. The cruise taken by the class of 1963 had a 21-day leg before it made its first port. (1955 *Tide Rips*.)

A CADET VISITING LONDON ON A LONG CRUISE. The class of 1963 had two long cruises. The first, in 1960, had liberty ports in Portsmouth, England; Oslo, Norway; and Le Havre, France. The first-class cruise in 1962 visited Edinburgh, Scotland; Antwerp, Belgium; and Las Palmas, in the Canary Islands. (1963 *Tide Rips*.)

A VISIT TO THE *EAGLE*. Mike and Julie Burdian (left) and Jan and Jan Smith from the class of 1963 are shown visiting the *Eagle*. The ship is in beautiful condition, considering that at the time of the publication of this book, she was 84 years old. (Courtesy of Mike Burdian.)

PRES. JOHN F. KENNEDY. The president made an official visit to the *Eagle* at the end of the 1962 long cruise. In charge of the honor guard is Cadet First Class Mike Burdian. Burdian had a successful 31-year career with IBM following his Coast Guard service. His son Steve (class of 1994) and daughter–in-law JoAnn (class of 1997) are both captains in the Coast Guard. (1963 *Tide Rips*.)

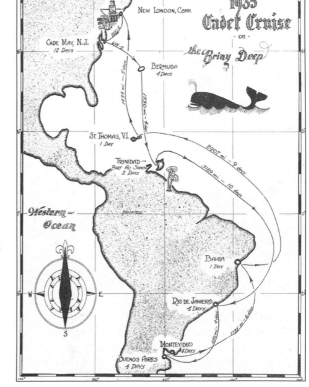

CHART OF 1935 LONG CRUISE. On this long cruise, port visits were made to Bermuda, Trinidad, Rio De Janeiro, Buenos Aires, Montevideo, Bahia, St. Thomas, and Cape May. There were 35 graduates in 1936, including future commandant Adm. Chester Bender, father of the modern single-breasted service uniform. (1936 *Tide Rips*.)

REEFING THE *EAGLE*'S SAILS. The cruises taught cadets the challenges of handling ships under sail. There are 145 different lines required to handle all of the *Eagle*'s sails. Third-class cadets were required to know the locations of them all. (1948 *Tide Rips*.)

LEADERSHIP 44 YACHTS. One of the most popular programs is the Coastal Sail Training Program, which occurs during the second-class summer. The program entails six to eight cadets and an assigned safety officer conducting a two-week sailing event, during which the duties of cook, deckhand, navigator, and crew chief are rotated. (Author's collection.)

COASTAL SAIL TRAINING PROGRAM CREW. Members rotate through all the positions. The program teaches the fundamentals of coastal sailing and leadership and followership principles. (Courtesy of the US Coast Guard Academy; photograph by PO2 Jordan Park.)

L44 YACHTS. Since the summer of 2013, the Coastal Sail Training Program has been done on eight yachts that were donated to the academy and cost approximately $1 million each. They are L44-01 *Shearwater*, sponsored by the class of 1953; L44-02 *Arctic Tern*, sponsored by the parents' association; L44-03 *Stormy Petrel*, sponsored by the class of 1958; L44-04 *Blue Goose*, sponsored by the Coast Guard Foundation; L44-05 *Osprey*, sponsored by the class of 1966; L44-06 *Seahawk*, sponsored by the class of 1960; L44-07 *Razorbill*, sponsored by the Coast Guard Foundation; and L44-08 *Egret*, sponsored by the Coast Guard Foundation. (Author's collection.)

MYSTIC FLAG DAY. One of the first events in which the new cadets are permitted to visit outside the academy campus is the Mystic Seaport Flag Day. This was the first liberty the author's class had in 1959, although they did not call it Flag Day then. The Mystic Seaport demonstrates the seafaring history of the New London area. In a recent addition, the incoming class has its flag dedicated each year. (Courtesy of the US Coast Guard Academy; photograph by PO3 Mathew Thieme.)

MARCHING IN PRES. DWIGHT D. EISENHOWER'S INAUGURATION. Every four years, the Academy Corps is transported to Washington, DC, to march in the inauguration. There is a lot of practice beforehand to ensure the military precision deserving of the event. The class of 1963 was honored to march in John F. Kennedy's inauguration in 1961. There was snow on the ground, and the cadets very nearly froze their feet in their low-cut dress oxfords. (1950 *Tide Rips*.)

PARADE IN NEW LONDON. The academy has been in the New London, Connecticut, area since 1910, when it moved to Fort Trumbull. Located midway between Boston and New York City, New London offers close proximity to large metro areas in an place with a rich seagoing history that makes for a nice fit. The community has been welcoming to the academy, including giving it a favorable price for its current location. (1954 *Tide Rips*.)

SPARS AT THE ACADEMY. On June 28, 1943, the first women became part of the academy when 50 officer candidates, the Coast Guard Women's Reserve, reported for indoctrination. However, they were only there for a streamlined six-week program—women did not actually become part of the regular academy until 1976. The name "SPARS" came from the first letters of the Coast Guard motto: "Semper Paratus, Always Ready." The Coast Guard Women's Reserve was established by Congress and signed into law by Pres. Franklin D. Roosevelt on November 23, 1942. (1944 *Tide Rips*.)

CADET FIRST CLASS JESSICA LUKASIK. In 2014, Lukasik was selected for the prestigious Fulbright Scholarship to study the fisheries and tourism industry on Mauritius, a small island nation some 1,200 miles off the coast of Africa. She would be studying at the University of Mauritius. The alumni association assists with funding for these important scholarships. (Courtesy of the US Coast Guard Academy; photograph by PO2 Cory Mendenhall.)

GUIDONS. Military formations continue from First Day to the Graduation Review. The guidons shown here in a lighter moment are used to line up the companies into regimental formations. (1952 *Tide Rips*.)

GEORGE WASHINGTON MONUMENT. This monument watches over the Washington Parade Ground. This statue is a bronze reproduction of the original statue of Washington created by French sculptor Jean-Antoine Houdon in 1792. The monument was dedicated by the class of 1969 on the occasion of their 50th homecoming. (Courtesy of Paul Duddy.)

WASHINGTON PARADE GROUND. The class of 2023 is pictured on July 1, 2019—their Swearing-In Day (or Day 1). This is the first day of Swab Summer, an exciting and intense seven-week training period that forms the foundation of each cadet's academy experience and military career. For parents, Swearing-In Day is a time to say goodbye and to let their son or daughter know that this is the beginning of a great adventure. (Courtesy of Paul Duddy.)

Six

PLAY

All work and no play make Jack a dull boy (or girl). They also make him (or her) out of shape. US Coast Guard Academy cadets are required to maintain a high standard of physical fitness. They are members of a military service. An enjoyable means of keeping fit is through regular participation in physical sports. An additional benefit of sports is building team spirit and fostering leadership. Despite the academy's relatively small size, which totals approximately 1,000 cadets, it has a surprising number of both male and female sports teams. In contrasting then and now, the scope of the athletic portion of the academy experience is perhaps the most different.

In 1932, the academy's first year at its present location, the *Tide Rips* yearbook listed only 5 sports: football, basketball, fencing, sailing, and boxing. Twenty years later, in 1952, there were 10 sports: football, basketball, swimming, wrestling, cross-country, track, baseball, rifle, pistol, and sailing. In 1963, there were 14 sports: football (that year's team became the first undefeated, untied academy team), soccer, cross-country, basketball, swimming, wrestling, pistol, rifle, hockey (which was dropped as a league sport after 1963), baseball, track, tennis, dinghies, and yachts.

In 2019, there were a total of 22 intercollegiate sports at the academy: baseball, men's basketball, women's basketball, men's crew, women's crew (ranked 12th nationally), men's cross-country (ranked 10th in New England), women's cross-country, dinghy sailing, football (ranked 2nd in the New England Men's and Women's Athletic Conference, or NEWMAC), men's indoor track, women's indoor track (Kaitlyn Mooney was the 5,000-meter national champion), men's lacrosse (NEWMAC champion), women's lacrosse, women's outdoor track, men's outdoor track, pistol, rifle, offshore sailing, men's soccer, women's soccer, softball, and women's volleyball.

In addition, the academy offers club sports: hockey, men's rugby, women's rugby, and triathlon. The alumni association financially supports these club sports. Adding to this impressive list are the following clubs: aviation, Cadets Against Sexual Assault (CASA), Sandhurst, dance, and water polo. Finally, there are the cultural councils: the Asian, Pacific, American Council; the Compañeros Club; the Genesis Club; the International Council Club; Spectrum (LGBTQ); and the Women's Leadership Initiative.

The academy's musical programs are an equally important component of cadet leisure activities. These include concert band, pep band, regimental band, Nite-Caps, Glee Club, Fair Winds, Idlers, and Windjammers.

COAST GUARD ACADEMY FOOTBALL SQUAD 1962

THE 1933 FOOTBALL TEAM. This sport has been played by Coast Guard cadets since 1922, starting at Fort Trumbull. This would have been the second team to play at the new academy. Billard Hall is visible in the background. (1934 *Tide Rips*.)

Dave Zwick, Co-captain; Otto Graham; Ed DeMuzzio, Co-captain

THE 1962 FOOTBALL TEAM. The 1962 team and coaches are pictured at the top of this image, with the bottom of the image featuring coach Otto Graham and cocaptains Dave Zwick (left) and Eddie DeMuzzio (right). This was Graham's third year as the academy's head football coach. In 1962, the team had five wins, two losses, and one tie. The next year, the team went undefeated. (1963 *Tide Rips*.)

A PERFECT SEASON. Coach Otto Graham is carried off the field following the last regular-season game in 1963. That year's team had a perfect record of 8–0. They held their opponents to only 42 total points for the season—an all-time academy record. (1964 *Tide Rips*.)

THE GOOD LUCK BABY. Coach Otto Graham (left) and cocaptain Bill Thompson kiss a baby following their perfect season in 1963. The child was the son of Capt. Joe Smith (class of 1956) and had attended nearly every game with his parents. The team considered him a good luck charm. (1964 *Tide Rips*.)

BIG GAIN AT JONES FIELD IN 1933. The original natural turf had a tendency to turn into a mud bowl during the rainy season. Note the leather helmets and lack of face guards. (1934 *Tide Rips.*)

THE 1954 PISTOL TEAM. While football gets a lot of attention, historically, the academy rifle and pistol teams are much more competitive on the national level. The teams practice in a modern indoor range in the basement of Chase Hall. The academy is a founding member of the New England Intercollegiate Rifle League, which held its first competition in New London in 1939. The academy's rifle team won the Mid-Atlantic Rifle Conference in 2019. (1954 *Tide Rips*.)

THE 1964 RIFLE TEAM. The first rifle team was formed at the academy in 1932. Mike Stenger (class of 1964), at farthest right in the first row, fired 200 out of a possible 200 in the Mohegan Rifle League Match in 1964. This was the first time that was ever accomplished by a cadet and only the second time it was ever done in competition. Stenger was an NRA master and went on to make captain, became an aviator, and commanded two air stations. (1964 *Tide Rips*.)

THE 1963 ICE HOCKEY TEAM. The Bears finished 2019 as the 11th-ranked team in the Atlantic Region in the regular season. US Coast Guard hockey has a long history that dates back to before World War II. At the academy, hockey is a club sport supported by the alumni association. In addition to the team's competitive Atlantic Coast Hockey Association league, active-duty and reserve members continue to play for years after graduating from the academy. The Coast Guard Hockey Organization helps promote league play, national armed forces and first responder tournaments, and the annual in-house Coast Guard Commandant's Cup ice hockey tournament in Cape Cod, Massachusetts. Playing hockey at the academy is the start of building skills and lifelong friendships within the Coast Guard hockey community. (1963 *Tide Rips*.)

KAITLYN MOONEY (CLASS OF 2021). Truly a running sensation, Mooney, nicknamed "Moon Man," was an All-American 2018 NEWMAC cross-country champion and Rookie of the Year in her fourth-class year. She ran the fastest time ever recorded for 5,000 meters in the Open New England Championship. She placed fourth at the national championship. (Courtesy of Paul Duddy.)

WOMEN'S BASKETBALL, 2018. Women's basketball consisted of 13 hardworking women on the team that had a record of 7 wins against 18 losses in 2018. Alex Ivansheck became the head coach of the academy team in 2012. She led the team to back-to-back 19-win seasons in 2013–2014 and 2014–2015. (Courtesy of the US Coast Guard Academy; Public Affairs.)

PEP RALLY, AUGUST 29, 2019. The T-shirts say "Respect, Honor, and Devotion to Duty." The swab bible, *The Running Light*, teaches that the answer to "What is respect?" is "valuing and appreciating the lives and sacrifices of others. The fundamental mission of the Coast Guard is saving lives and by having respect for the lives of all people, the leaders of our organization are able to accomplish our core mission." (Courtesy of Paul Duddy.)

HELEN OH AND BRIAN KIM (CLASS OF 2019). The two shooters display their national championship rings for pistol. The 2019 US Coast Guard Academy pistol team won the NRA Collegiate Pistol National Championship and had a 12–1 match record. This picture was taken in both cadets' third-class year. Both of them graduated in 2019 with over 20 national titles between them. (Courtesy of Paul Duddy.)

PRACTICING FOR THE OLYMPICS. Brian Kim and Helen Oh have kept up their practicing even after graduation. They are assigned to the academy and practice their shooting each day; they are hoping to make the next Olympic team. (Courtesy of Paul Duddy.)

ALL-AMERICAN ANITA GREEN (CLASS OF 2019). Green was the regimental commander, the top cadet of the academy. She was part of the 4/800 women's relay team that set the all-time academy record and was fourth all-time for Division III. Cadet First Class Green was the cocaptain of the women's cross-country team. In the 2019 *Tide Rips*, she wrote that she and her cocaptain Nina Ragle had been blessed with the love that the team shared with each other. (Courtesy of Paul Duddy.)

REGIMENTAL COMMANDER ANITA GREEN. Below, Green is pictured escorting visiting dignitaries during an academy review. She was the second African American female regimental commander. Her major was mechanical engineering. She is from Clermont, Florida, and after graduating in 2019, she was assigned to the cutter *Decisive* in Pensacola, Florida. (Courtesy of US Coast Guard Academy Public Affairs.)

BOXING AT THE ACADEMY. This was one of the five sports played at Fort Trumbull. Boxing has been an off-and-on team sport at the academy. As of this writing, in summer 2020, the boxing ring on the third deck of the Alumni Center has been dismantled for lack of a coach and safety concerns of the senior administration. (1932 *Tide Rips*.)

BOXING TEAM, 1934. The recent academy teams, with a volunteer coach and boxing being just a club, still had five collegiate national champions, 30 All-Americans, four Golden Glove champs, and two Olympic team trial qualifiers. The team placed as high as third in the country. (1934 *Tide Rips*.)

2019 ACADEMY BASEBALL TEAM. Six members of the team were selected for the NEWMAC All-Star Team. The seniors in this photograph are holding pictures summarizing their careers. (Courtesy of Paul Dudley.)

OLYMPIC HOPEFULS. Lt. (jg) Nikole Barnes (class of 2017), who is at the tiller, finished as the highest-ranked team in the 2018 World Sailing Championship in Aarhus, Denmark. While at the academy, Barnes was named the Women Sailor of the Year for College Sailing for 2015–2016 and All-American for both women's and coed sailing during her sophomore and junior years, with an honorable mention in her freshman year. She was named Female Rookie of the Year and was recognized as the College Women's Sailor of the Year in 2016. (Courtesy of Paul Duddy.)

NIKOLE BARNES (CLASS OF 2017). Barnes (center) is pictured with Rear Adm. Rudy Peschel, US Coast Guard (retired), and the author (left) at an alumni association appreciation dinner. These dinners are important to recognize those partners who are making a significant contribution to the academy. Typically, they are held in conjunction with an alumni board of directors meeting. Outstanding cadet leaders and athletes, like Barnes, are also invited. (Author's collection.)

DINGHY SAILING COMPETITION ON THE THAMES RIVER. The dinghy team is one of the most competitive teams at the academy, with a winning tradition in some of the toughest regattas in the country. Many academy sailors have been named All-Americans, and the Coast Guard Academy Alumni Bowl is awarded every spring to the winning team at the New England Dinghy Championship. (Courtesy of Paul Duddy.)

DINGHY SAILING IN THE 1940s. Note the absence of the academy's current buildings, such as Roland Hall. The Thames River is shared with the submarines that are based upriver in Groton. Once, a cadet, while sailing, made a surfaced submarine back down under strict rules of the road that give sail the right of way over power. The cadet was subsequently given a class-one offense for embarrassing the Navy. (1943 *Tide Rips*.)

ACADEMY SWIM TEAM, 1940. Swimming is a mandatory sport at the academy. Sailors must be able to swim, and swimming is at the core of the physical education curriculum. (1940 *Tide Rips*.)

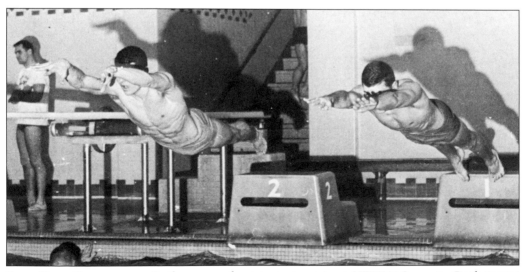

SWIM TEAM COMPETITION. Both men and women compete at NEWMAC meets. Both teams routinely have All-American and All-Conference swimmers. (1966 *Tide Rips*.)

BILLARD HALL. This building was named for Commandant Frederick C. Billard, who was instrumental in authorizing $1.75 million in Congress for the secretary of the treasury to start the process that resulted in the academy's move from Fort Trumbull to its present location. For years, Billard Hall was the center for academy sports. It now contains the Otto Graham Center for Athletic Excellence. (1940 *Tide Rips*.)

SAILING ON THE THAMES. This is one of the eight beautiful Leadership 44 yachts that received funding from the alumni association in 2013. These yachts enable the entire second-class year to experience coastal sailing in an intimate team-building setting. The Coastal Sail Training Program is one of the most popular programs at the academy. (Courtesy of Paul Duddy.)

WOMAN'S EIGHT-PERSON SHELL. The rowing center supporting this program was dedicated in 1982, as was the Seamanship Sailing Center in 1984. The Coast Guard Academy Alumni Association and the Coast Guard Foundation jointly funded both projects. (Courtesy of Paul Duddy.)

WOMEN'S SOFTBALL. Cadet Hayley Feindel (left; class of 2012) talks with the superintendent, Rear Adm. Sandra Stosz (1982), the first female academy graduate to be selected for flag rank. Admiral Stosz was herself a champion athlete, having won the Maryland State Female Discus Championship in 1977 when she was a student at Mount Hebron High School. Feindel was an All-American softball pitcher. Over the course of her four years at the academy, she led the women's softball team to four straight NCAA tournament playoff berths. She also led the team to three NEWMAC titles (in 2010, 2011, and 2012) and was NEWMAC Pitcher of the Year three times. Her most impressive feats as an athlete at the academy included 17 individual school records and the NCAA Division 3 record for all-time strikeouts (1,457). Among those school records are her single-season ERA (0.56) and complete games (140). (Courtesy of Paul Duddy.)

CROSS-COUNTRY. In this picture, the 2019 team members are being recognized at a ceremony on the plaza of the Roland Center. Seniors are given pictures to commemorate their involvement with the team. (Author's collection.)

ACADEMY WRESTLING TEAM. The team had a record of 9–3 in 2018. Nick Remke (class of 2019) and Owen McClave (class of 2020) were All-Americans that year. (Courtesy of Paul Duddy.)

CADET MUSICAL. Music is an important aspect of cadet recreational activities. Academy bands include the concert band, pep band, regimental band, Nite-Caps, Glee Club, Fair Winds, Idlers, and Windjammers. (Courtesy of Paul Duddy.)

CADET IDLERS. Eight members of the class of 1959 formed this all-male a cappella singing group in 1957 on the summer cruise. The academy band director took interest and expanded the repertoire of the group. The group has performed at the White House for Pres. Dwight D. Eisenhower and his wife, Mamie; at Carnegie Hall; and on *Saturday Night Live*. (1969 *Tide Rips*.)

Seven

PARTNERS

At the academy, many of the most popular activities outside of academics require funding beyond that provided by the appropriated budget. The academy must compete with all of the operational programs of the Coast Guard for its share of the pie. Unfortunately, the Coast Guard has not always been a top priority for federal dollars. To be competitive for the quality student the academy desires, it is critical that it be as attractive an option as possible. These special features are often referred to as the margin of excellence. In 2019, the alumni association provided $4.7 million to the academy. The alumni association is just one of the partners for the academy.

Over the years, these features and programs have grown significantly. Some are practical, such as funding the state-of-the-art turf for Jones Field, a gift of the class of 1953. When the field was natural grass, it would turn into a mud bowl when it got wet.

Another enhancement—in an entirely different direction—is the endowed chair for the Center for Arctic Study and Policy. The chair was possible largely thanks to a $1 million commitment from the class of 1965. Alumni are definitely important partners.

The Parents Giving Program directly supports initiatives targeted at enhancing cadet life. An example is the $1 million Cadet Strength and Conditioning Center, which will be an 8,000-square-foot facility with the latest equipment.

The Coast Guard Foundation is another important partner. Capt. George W. Holtzman (class of 1933) founded it in 1969 as a nonprofit organization to support academy projects. It has funded several major efforts, such as Crown Park, three of the Leadership 44 yachts, the rowing center, and many other initiatives. In 1986, the Coast Guard Foundation expanded to provide support for the entire Coast Guard family.

Partners are important in strengthening relationships. The Coast Guard Academy Affinity Councils recognize and foster diversity. They started in 1973 as the Genesis Council, which encourages understanding of the African American community. This was followed by Compañeros (originally ANSO), which fosters understanding of those of Hispanic heritage. The International Council was formed in 2004 to stress understanding and build relationships with foreign cultures, especially international sea services. The Asian Pacific American Council was created in 2004 to further cadets' international awareness. The Women's Leadership Council was formed in 2011, followed by the Spectrum Council, which supports LGBTQ+ people, in 2012.

WOMEN'S LEADERSHIP INITIATIVE. This luncheon was held in the Otto Graham Hall of Athletic Excellence. The Women's Leadership Initiative was established in 2012 as a partner with the alumni association to support leadership training and professional development opportunities for Coast Guard women both in uniform and civilians. It has two goals: to increase retention of women in the Coast Guard and to provide a bridge for female service personnel to achieve success following their Coast Guard careers. The Women's Leadership Council was formed in 2011 to promote female health and wellness, create a professional leadership network, and allow positive associations between male and female cadets. (Courtesy of Paul Duddy.)

THE *EAGLE* ENTERING SYDNEY HARBOR. In 1988, the *Eagle* was sent to Australia as the US representative for Australia's centennial celebration. As it is now approaching nearly a century of operational life, the *Eagle* requires extensive TLC. The alumni association, led by the class of 1978, recently completed projects on the ship totaling $230,000 in 2016. (Courtesy of Ernie Cummings [class of 1963].)

SATELLITE COMMUNICATIONS GROUND STATION. This dome is located on the roof of Smith Hall. The 18-foot-diameter geodesic dome was established as a joint partnership of the Coast Guard Research and Development Center and the Department of Homeland Security Science and Technology Polar Scout Project. It joins with a similar Coast Guard Research and Development station in Fairbanks, Alaska. The primary goal is to see whether these small satellites can augment the National Oceanic and Atmospheric Administration's system of larger satellites that collect data from search-and-rescue beacons in the Arctic. NOAA's system is nearing the end of its service life. The Coast Guard has said the satellites could also be used to track sea ice in the Arctic, reducing the cost of operating Coast Guard aircraft, which mainly carry out this work, and the risk to aircrews. (Author's collection.)

ALUMNI CENTER BRICK PLAZA. An innovative fundraiser is located in the plaza on the Jones Field side of the Alumni Center, where special bricks can be dedicated to or by individuals for a $1,000 per brick. This generates approximately $60,000 each year and provides a very special place for visitors and alumni to reflect. The author's brick is visible in this image. (Author's collection.)

THE BEAR CLUB. Operating under the umbrella of the Coast Guard Academy Alumni Association, the Bear Club provides critical financial support to academy athletics for cadet athletic travel, retaining coaches in non-billeted positions, and cadet athletic recruiting. The budget for academy athletics in 2016 was $296,219. The Bear Club supports all 25 varsity and 5 club sports—in 2016, these club sports included boxing, hockey, rugby, triathlon, and water polo. A special Bear Club program was the football reunion in December 2019. The class of 1958, the Otto Graham Athletic Legacy Fund, and the 1963 championship football team funded the press box. (Courtesy of Paul Duddy.)

OTTO GRAHAM GOLF CLASSIC. This annual event, which started in 2008, has been hosted at premier golf courses around the country. It has raised over $265,000 to support Coast Guard Academy athletics. In this picture, two alumni from the class of 1963, Ed DeMuzzio (left) and Mike Studley (right), stand with golf legend Arnold Palmer, who has been a supporter of the event and was enlisted in the Coast Guard prior to beginning his amazing golf career. (Courtesy of Ed DeMuzzio.)

BOB LEGGETT (CLASS OF 1963) AND BILL THOMPSON (CLASS OF 1964). Both Leggett and Thompson are members of the Academy Athletic Hall of Fame. Thompson (right) was instrumental in conceiving and starting the Otto Graham Golf Classic. (Courtesy of Bob Leggett.)

AFRICAN AMERICAN GRADUATES, CLASS OF 2019. Academy Affinity Councils are important partners that are committed to striving to excel, fostering unity, and instilling respect in the academy. Pictured are the African American graduates in the class of 2019. (Courtesy of Paul Duddy.)

THE GRAHAM FAMILY. Football coach Otto Graham was a partner as the advisor to the class of 1964. Here, he is pictured (at far right) with his wife, Beverly, and their children. Graham is holding a mounted broom symbolizing the clean sweep of the undefeated 1963 season. (1964 *Tide Rips*.)

Eight

PREPARED

The first chapter emphasized the mission of the academy to:

> Graduate young men and women of sound bodies, stout hearts and alert minds, with a liking for the sea and its lore and with that high sense of honor, loyalty and obedience which goes with trained initiative and leadership; well-grounded in seamanship, the sciences, and the humanities, and strong in the resolve to be worthy of the traditions of commissioned officers in the United States Coast Guard in the service of their country and humanity.

This could be summarized as "graduate officers prepared to effectively serve." Admittedly, the author is biased, but he feels that the academy is doing a fine job.

The Coast Guard that modern graduates enter is much more complicated than in earlier years. It seems that if something occurs on the water, the Coast Guard is responsible for its safety and success. As the Arctic becomes more accessible due to global warming, the Coast Guard, as the principal federal presence and the only service with icebreakers, will face new challenges. The Jarvis Overland Rescue serves to remind people that the Arctic presents dangers for the unprepared.

The class of 2019 is unquestionably more prepared than the class of 1963 was when they graduated. Graduates in 2019 included 19 electrical engineering, 29 mechanical engineering, 32 civil engineering, 17 naval architecture and marine engineering, 31 marine and environmental sciences, 29 operations research and computer analysis, 38 management, and 50 government majors.

The world they face includes challenges the class of 1963 could only imagine. Global terrorism is a concern for all nations. More countries have nuclear capabilities. There are many more humans competing for the earth's resources. The mix of potential problems will only increase.

Throughout nearly 150 years, US Coast Guard Academy graduates have had to be ready to step into challenging, complex, and critical situations in which they must be able to perform with competence. Now, they are entering positions of responsibility for the safety of mankind, efficient operation of maritime commerce, protection of the environment, and security of their nation. It is to the credit of the academy and its staff that they have always done just that. It is the alumni's responsibility to see to it that they are *Semper Paratus*—Always Prepared.

GRADUATION, 1963. Gold stripes and heavy responsibility are placed on the graduate's shoulders. Steve Ulmer (1963) has his ensign shoulder boards attached by his mother. Two years after this happy time, he was at war. (Courtesy of Steve Ulmer.)

THE VIETNAM WAR. An 82-foot Coast Guard patrol boat is pictured in battle dress. Thirty-one members of the class of 1963 were serving in Vietnam within two years of their graduation. (Courtesy of Jim Furaus.)

T/V *Exxon Valdez* Off-loading Oil. The service, with its 11 different mission areas, presents the opportunity for challenges in many arenas. The grounding of the *Exxon Valdez* on March 24, 1989, which resulted in an ecological disaster in a pristine area of Alaska, is a worst-case scenario. The cleanup, which went on for three years, had the Coast Guard as the federal on scene commander (FOSC). Political pressure saw the responsibility for FOSC escalate from the captain of Port Valdez to the district commander and, finally, to the area commander, Vice Adm. Clyde Robbins, who was headquartered in Alameda, California. (Courtesy of US Coast Guard District 17.)

Search and Rescue. Recent academy graduates are going directly to flight training with the Navy in Pensacola, Florida. Pictured is an HH-65 with a rescue swimmer. Helicopters with flight crews and swimmers from around the Coast Guard were detailed to New Orleans after Hurricane Katrina struck land there. There were over 1,800 total fatalities and property damage that totaled a record $125 billion. The service was ultimately credited with saving 33,000 lives. (Author's collection.)

HEALY. The icebreaker *Healy* is shown at the North Pole. There is a critical need for additional icebreakers as activities in the Arctic increase. Many graduates will accordingly see icebreaker duty in their careers. Alaska, the "last frontier," will become of more and more importance to the service and the nation. (Courtesy of USCGC *Healy*.)

BEAR IN THE ICE. Despite climate change and a warming planet, ice will still come, and it will be unpredictable, moving with wind and current. Icebreakers will still be needed to work the Arctic and support the Antarctic. (Courtesy of University of Alaska–Fairbanks.)

THE ICEBREAKER *EASTWIND* IN THE ICE. The seven Wind-class icebreakers, like the *Eastwind*, have all been decommissioned but will likely be replaced in the future. New ensigns can expect to have them as assignment potentials. (Courtesy of US Coast Guard Commandant Public Relations.)

GUNNERY DRILL. Ens. Bob Kuhnle (class of 1963) is pictured on the 40-millimeter mount on the USCGC *Pontchartrain* on Ocean Station November. The majority of academy graduates are assigned to cutters. For the class of 1963, many of these afloat assignments were on ocean station vessels (OSV) at the midway point of transoceanic air routes. The jobs were typically gunnery officer, communications officer, or first lieutenant. Kuhnle eventually went to flight training and was selected as the outstanding flight student for 1966. He later earned a doctorate from Old Dominion University. (Author's collection.)

OCEAN STATION VESSEL. An OSV launches a weather balloon in this painting by Tony Falcone that is on display in the Alumni Center activity room. This painting shows the USCGC *Casco* on Ocean Station Bravo. From the 1950s into the 1970s, the Coast Guard manned four ocean stations in the Atlantic and two in the Pacific. In addition to taking weather observation, they were located on the midway point in oceanic routes as a safety measure. Two aircraft actually ditched, and passengers were saved by the OSVs. Many members of the class of 1963 were assigned to OSVs. Satellite weather data gathering and improvements in airplane safety eliminated the need for the OSV program in the 1970s. This painting was sponsored by the class of 1955. (Author's collection.)

BUOY-TENDING OPERATIONS. This painting by Mike Koloski (class of 1965) is also in the Alumni Center activities room. The Coast Guard is responsible for maintaining 97,000 short-range aids to navigation, including beacons, buoys, lighthouses, ranges, and sound signals. The scope is extensive, with 25,000 miles of navigable waters and nearly 95,000 miles of coastline. Many graduates will report to the black hulls of the buoy tender fleet. When the class of 1963 graduated, these were considered plum assignments because of the opportunity for extensive ship-handling and small wardrooms. (Author's collection.)

HH-60T Jayhawk. The nickname for this helicopter is the "Big Iron." The Coast Guard had 42 operational Jayhawks in 2020. Unlike in earlier classes, when all graduates were assigned afloat, recent graduates have been assigned directly to sectors, to other shore billets, and to flight training. All initial flight training is done with the Naval Education and Training Command in Pensacola, Florida. (Courtesy of the US Coast Guard.)

Polar Star in Antarctica. This mural by Tony Falcone is on display in the Alumni Center activities room and was sponsored by the class of 1955. The *Polar Star* is the Coast Guard's only operational Polar-class icebreaker. Every year, the resupply of the research station at McMurdo Sound is a priority. Upcoming graduates of the academy can expect icebreaker assignments for the foreseeable future. (Author's collection.)

THE CLASS OF 1963 CELEBRATES THEIR 50TH REUNION. This picture was taken following the Medallion Ceremony. Classes form very tight bonds that continue throughout their lives. In this case, three-quarters of all living classmates who graduated in 1963 came back to the academy to receive 50-year medallions from the commandant, Adm. Robert Papp (class of 1975). This class was well prepared. The 93 graduates earned 104 master's degrees and seven doctorates. Three made flag rank. The class commanded 129 units afloat and ashore. Ten became lawyers, two became ordained ministers, and seventeen earned wings. Thirty-one went to Vietnam, earning 14 Bronze Stars and 3 Silver Stars among them. (Author's collection.)

PLAQUE AT ENTRANCE TO CHASE HALL. Graduates are prepared to enter the Long Blue Line with this motto foremost in their mind. From their first entry into the academy through the end of their four years, they have lived this motto. According to the words of welcome in *The Running Lights*, "The Academy is an intense crucible designed to break down, purify, and re-forge your class into the best version of itself. Rely on your shipmates, and look to them for strength, for you cannot succeed without them." (Author's collection.)

FOURTH CLASS SHOULDER BOARD CEREMONY. It is a long, hard road to this ceremony signifying the transition from swab to fourth class to the ensign shoulder boards at graduation. As *The Running Lights* states: "Every member of the Long Blue Line has stared into the eyes of service and sacrifice and has not blinked. Will you?" (Courtesy of Paul Duddy.)

THE ACADEMY OF TODAY. As shown in this image looking north along Bear Drive, the appearance of the academy has changed little, but the officers it produces are entering a more complex world of terrorism, environmental challenges, and increasing dependence on the ocean for commerce. (1940 *Tide Rips*.)

PARENTS AND FRIENDS AT THE SHOULDER BOARD CEREMONY. Many people assist cadets in preparing them to become successful Coast Guard officers. Cadets should make sure these supporters know how much their contributions to the nation's future are appreciated. (Courtesy of Paul Duddy.)

CADET FORMAL DANCE. The partners that cadets choose to accompany them in their careers will also accept a challenging life. The author and his family moved 15 times during his 30 years of active duty. It meant leaving behind many old friends and starting over at many new schools. Legendary World War II naval leader Adm. Chester Nimitz's wife, when asked about her memories of her husband's illustrious career, replied, "Buying and leaving garbage cans all around the world." (1942–1943 *Tide Rips*.)

PRES. JOHN F. KENNEDY MEMORIAL FLAG CEREMONY. The shooting of President Kennedy in 1963 seemed to signal the vulnerability of the country to attacks by nontraditional means. The impact on the preparedness of graduates charged with the security of ports is considerable. (1964 *Tide Rips*.)

1960 COLOR GUARD. During times of uncertainty, tradition, ceremony, and symbols can be reassuring. The knowledge that many before them have gone into uncertain times can give cadets the courage to do their part. (1961 *Tide Rips*.)

CADETS MARCHING IN SNOW. These cadets are marching into a different and challenging future. From the beginning of the Revenue Cutter Service, when it had a single mission of collecting taxes, the Coast Guard has grown to include a complex mix of 11 statutory missions that entail the protection of lives, property, and national security. (1950 *Tide Rips*.)

ALEXANDER HAMILTON STATUE. Alexander Hamilton looks to the flag and the future. The founder of the Coast Guard is positioned looking across the parade ground toward his mentor Pres. George Washington. (Courtesy of and photograph by Lorna Andrews.)

Discover Thousands of Local History Books
Featuring Millions of Vintage Images

Arcadia Publishing, the leading local history publisher in the United States, is committed to making history accessible and meaningful through publishing books that celebrate and preserve the heritage of America's people and places.

Find more books like this at
www.arcadiapublishing.com

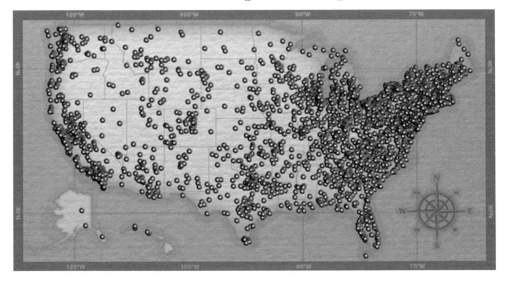

Search for your hometown history, your old stomping grounds, and even your favorite sports team.

Consistent with our mission to preserve history on a local level, this book was printed in South Carolina on American-made paper and manufactured entirely in the United States. Products carrying the accredited Forest Stewardship Council (FSC) label are printed on 100 percent FSC-certified paper.

MADE IN THE USA